Some Sense About Wilhelm Reich

Some Sense About Wilhelm Reich

Leo Raditsa

PHILOSOPHICAL LIBRARY
NEW YORK

Published, 1978, by Philosophical Library, Inc.,
15 East 40 Street, New York, N. Y. 10016
Copyright 1978 by Leo Raditsa
All rights reserved
Library of Congress Catalog Card No. 77-009222
SBN 8022-2212-9
Manufactured in the United States of America

FOR LARISSA

Messieurs, je ne viens pas prêcher la tolérance. La Liberté la plus illimitée de religion est à mes yeux un droit si sacré, que le mot tolérance, qui voudrait l'exprimer, me parait en quelque sorte tyrannique lui-même; puisque l'existence de l'autorité, qui a le pouvoir de tolérer, attente à la liberté de penser, par cela même qu'elle tolère, et qu'ainsi elle pourrait ne pas tolérer.

Mirabeau

Contents

Preface	11
Introduction	17
Theory	
Therapy	25
Energy	43
Politics	49
Experience	
Therapy	57
Energy	79
Politics	85
Work and Life: Conclusions	99
Footnotes	119

Preface

My wife, Larissa Bonfante, suggested I write this essay in 1975 when I was struggling to come to terms with Wilhelm Reich's influence on me. It was the obvious thing to do but it had not occurred to me. Joel Carmichael and Gertrude Himmelfarb took the time to read the manuscript and make criticisms. They gave me courage. I thank them warmly.

Leo Raditsa

July, 1977
London

Some Facts

Wilhelm Reich was born on March 24, 1897 in Dobrycynica, in the part of Galicia then in the Austro-Hungarian Empire. In 1915 he earned his *Abitur*; in 1916 he entered the Austro-Hungarian army as an officer. He matriculated at the University of Vienna in 1918 and graduated in 1922 with a degree in medicine. From 1922 to 1930 Reich was first clinical assistant and then (in 1928) vice director of Freud's Psychoanalytic Polyclinic. In addition from 1924-1930 Reich directed the Seminar for Psychoanalytic Therapy, the training institute for psychoanalysts. In 1927 the first edition of *The Function of the Orgasm* appeared, in 1928 an article on character analysis, which was to grow into the book, *Character Analysis*, first published in 1933. In 1927 Reich came into conflict with Freud; in 1928 he joined the Austrian Communist Party; and in 1929 he visited the Soviet Union briefly. In September 1930 Reich left Vienna for Berlin. In March 1933 he left Germany for Scandinavia where he grew disillusioned with the Communist party, some time before it expelled him. Some time after, in August 1934, the International Psychoanalytic Association took a series of actions against Reich which amounted to expulsion. Reich left Oslo for the United States in August, 1939. A little after his arrival in the United States, in 1940, Reich built the first accumulator for Orgone energy. During the years 1954-1957 he was prosecuted by the Federal Government. He was sentenced to two years' imprisonment for violation of a Federal injunction May 25, 1956. He entered a Federal penitentiary on March 12, 1957 and died in prison on November 3, a few days before he was scheduled for a parole hearing.

He was married three times; he had two daughters from his first wife and a son from his third wife, Ilse Ollendorff Reich.

Main source: Ilse Ollendorff Reich, *Wilhelm Reich: A Personal Biography*, New York, 1969.

INTRODUCTION

INTRODUCTION

I say some sense about Wilhelm Reich, because it would be arrogant of me to claim I could arrive at common sense about Reich. I do not think common sense is to be achieved now.

The situation concerning Reich is not a good one. His works sell a great deal all over the free world. But in the United States, at least, they are not discussed much. People swear by him or dismiss him, but they cannot speak about him critically. They either wish him away or fervently yearn for him to conquer. This is bothersome. For each attitude, either wholesale dismissal or wholesale acceptance, is evasive.

I have studied Reich's work for almost twenty years. I first read him in the middle fifties just after graduating from college. At that time Reich was more or less a forbidden author. Banned by court order, his books were not for sale, and generally difficult to get hold of. They were usually either missing from the major libraries or had never been acquired in the first place. Reich's influence on the radical thinkers I was then drawn to, like Paul Goodman or John Hurkan, was palpable. Reich seemed to be always in the background, the thinker nobody could cope with or convincingly dismiss. He is still that now. Even several of my undergraduate teachers whose tolerance for almost everything looked to me much like indifference automatically unleashed their scorn at the mention of Reich. Without such an author, whom you read knowingly, at your own risk and in secret, you cannot have an education, that is learn that thinking needs courage and runs dangers.

When I did read Reich I had the overwhelming sense that everything he said was true or should be true. I had the sense that he understood everything—that here was the truth, here was the answer. It did not occur to me to question this feeling. Perhaps the point of such feelings is that one does not question them.

One of Freud's most able students, perhaps the only one of Freud's students who knew how to become something other than a disciple and yet remain true to the essentials of Freud's discoveries, Reich, whatever else he did, addressed important questions in high earnestness, questions such as the relation of sexuality (I mean love) to freedom, questions which have become the common clap-trap of the day, that is questions which we cannot address earnestly and yet no longer know how to leave gracefully and decently alone. I mean our obsessions.

This strange situation in which Reich is read fervently but not discussed openly—and in which, incidentally, Reich's ideas circulate widely without being attributed to him—is in part Reich's doing. In some sense Reich divided the world into those who were for him or against him. At the same time he tried, it is true, to keep before his eyes the indifferent and for the most part helpless good will of the majority, but not in a way that now convinces me. For he would not talk to anyone who was not ready beforehand to agree with him—or at least suspend all disbelief in his presence. In fact he went to the point of insisting that no one could understand his work who had not been his patient or undergone his therapy. In the end such an attitude put Reich in a situation, as he remarked heartbreakingly to his friend A.S. Neill, where he had no friends, only patients.[1]

For years I took the obviously defensive reactions of repulsion to Reich's work the way he took them. In his view they betrayed the incapacity of many people to face unpleasant truths about themselves and take responsibility for their lives. In the hard progress of experience I have, however, begun to credit these hard gut reactions of distrust for Reich's work with a core of rationality. There is plenty of cowardice in them and, in the case of some, viciousness, but they also bespeak prudence and a fairly admirable awareness that whatever individuals can do for themselves, they will have to do themselves.

Reich's own occasional, fairly contemptuous lashing-out at the average man's, in his eyes, pathetic and stubborn clinging to his defenses points to some realization on his part that this apparent stubbornness of refusal was not entirely irrational, that the "no" which the average man almost involuntarily showed his work had something genuine about it. Something, that is, that could not be denied.

Reich's reluctance to look this negative reaction to his work in the face increased his dangerous isolation. In its turn this isolation made him exaggeratedly touchy about criticism and magnified his readiness to explain away all resistance to his discoveries as irrational. He spoke with passion of the frequent indifference to great work and of how even recognition, official praise and the like, often amounted to a powerful way of dismissing what one ostensibly admired. But the words are hollow, the passion does not reach conviction. I do not think he convinced himself with these explanations. In fact I think they only increased his doubts.

In any case in the long run it was his friends, his apparent friends, or as he called them his patients, who did Reich the most damage. Most of all by submitting him to an apparent worship which invited madness. Reich realized this, of course, and gave a great deal of thought to the destructiveness of discipleship, discipleship which I think he hungered after and at the same time regretted.

He saw acutely that discipleship led almost inevitably to betrayal. The man who led the FDA prosecution against him in 1954 had been his lawyer. An associate of his informed the government that Reich was violating the federal injunction against renting orgone boxes in interstate commerce. Worse still, none of his collaborators, none of those, that is, who thought they loved his work, had the presence of mind and courage to convince Reich that to ignore Federal prosecution was not a rational way to fight it.[2]

In the name of the courage of going to the roots Reich expected individuals to yield to his understanding beforehand. He could not imagine *bona fide* disagreement or objection. Since he had discovered the truth there was no room for disagreement with it or with him—he hardly distinguished between the two. He expected individuals to take the hard things he had to say without discussion. But at the same time he complained that few serious people listened to him or would hold discourse with him. I do not think he would face the consequences of his defiance.

Like many intellectuals and perhaps also many revolutionaries Reich wanted it both ways. He wanted to break the rules himself but expected others to stick to them. He wanted to tell people in no uncertain terms what they were, to mock common decency and call it mere hypocrisy, but at the same time he expected to continue to enjoy this decency, to continue to taste the old-time fairness, respect, good manners and grace.

He wanted both, he wanted the old-time fairness but he also wanted people to be free to be themselves. In fact, unless they were free to be their true selves they would never, in his view, be truly decent. As far as he was concerned his harshness, his insistence on saying it all, really amounted to no more than a test of decency. He wanted to make sure it was not "mere" convention: he had to test it. He could not take it for granted. He could not experience it without first having tested it. Maybe he feared to experience it.

This refusal to face the consequences of defiance is typical of our time, of the time, that is, after the First World War. Perhaps in its public posturings (which have little to do with how constructive people actually accomplish their lives) no time has taken defiance so lightly, been so mindless of its consequences. I mean the paralysis and blindness and finally destructiveness likely to follow upon compulsive or "idealistic" defiance, that is defiance directed in general at the whole "system," in distinction to the "no" which arises of its own in the face of an actual wrong. The "no" which names names and allows for "personal" (as if there were any other!) responsibility.

Such defiance which undermines the right of opposition and criticism exercises fascination, because it appears to provide complete assurance. It has the answers. The apparent answers can be overwhelmingly attractive in a world that reminds you constantly that no one will tell you what you must tell yourself, where there is little apparent fundamental agreement about anything, even about the most elemental matters, such as the distinction between freedom and slavery or between aggression and self-defense, where men fear to believe what they can see with their own eyes and so are ashamed of what they think—and where, as a result, there is a constant danger that the most crucial distinctions will have to be drawn in war, because they cannot be drawn when there are few hostilities but no peace.

But Reich, in contrast to most so-called radical thinkers, managed always to keep ahead of his answers. He kept on asking questions. He kept on learning although he increasingly would not let anybody teach him, except for little children, of whom he spoke movingly as the greatest teachers. It is often hard to tell which was deeper in him: his love of life, by which he meant nature untouched by man, or his disgust for what man had made of it. Hard to tell whether he loved nature so much because he hated man, or raged at what man had made of himself because he loved nature. Such power as he exercises comes from his capacity to make some individuals realize the extent of their self-betrayal, their distance from nature and themselves.

THEORY

Therapy

Reich's most important early work consisted in focusing on the transference relationship between patient and therapist. Faced with evidence in the twenties that psychoanalysis led to self-understanding but not to cure, Reich began to look at the relationship between therapist and patient in order to understand what impeded healing. As he looked he noticed that patients who seemed superficially and exaggeratedly cooperative actually gave all sorts of oblique indications of their hostility to him and therapy. They arrived late for treatment, one patient shook his head to indicate disagreement even as he assured Reich in words that he agreed with his observation, another obviously said what he thought was expected of him, i.e. used his knowledge of pyschoanalysis as a defense.

Instead of ignoring all these indications as had usually been the case, Reich decided to address them head-on.

Reich reasoned that the hidden defiance of the patients kept them from taking the therapy and the therapist seriously enough to be healed. By bringing this defiance into the open, Reich wanted to create a situation in which the patient could be completely open about everything, including his feelings towards his therapist. He thus broke with the psychoanalytic tradition that held that a therapist should quietly wait upon the patient's self-realization.

This attack on the surface, this readiness to interfere directly with the surface, with what the patient was feeling in the here and now, led Reich to major discoveries. He noticed that when he got a patient finally to express what he really meant, often some involuntary physical expression would occur, like a flushing in the face or shaking or pallor. At times these symptoms would be followed by a startling relinquishment of mannerisms, for instance an individual would of his own suddenly drop the fawning he had been given to. Or a patient who had been unable to stop chattering would come to keep his silence.

The indication that words, especially words that hit the mark, could evince strong physical reactions made Reich pause. It seemed to point to a direct relation or interplay between the realm of the soul and the body.

Most importantly, Reich noticed that marked inhibition of breathing occurred, especially on inspiration, when patients suppressed some emotion. He hit upon the notion of encouraging patients to breathe just at the moment when they appeared to be clamping down on themselves. When he did this on some occasions emotions would occur, especially of anger, and memories would follow quickly *after* them, memories of childhood incidents in which the patient had been humiliated and threatened into suppressing his anger.

Gradually, very gradually, Reich conceived the idea that the set of a person's body, for instance, if he held his chest in a more or less chronic attitude of inspiration, could tell him a great deal of his attitude toward life. He wondered if attacking bodily defenses as well as mental defenses would not provide a powerful tool for getting at a patient's troubles. If, for instance, he encouraged a person whose breathing was markedly inhibited to breathe, would not this be a more powerful way to getting at the past than through talk? Talking, in psychoanalysis, had managed to bring patients to an understanding of themselves that had, however, not brought with it any emotion, any release of affect. In Reich's conception, the actual past, especially the unresolved past, lay caged both in the body, in the tensions of the muscles, which expressed a person's set toward life, as well as in his mental and spiritual attitudes.

As he began to work in this direction Reich gradually discovered that everyday expressions of speech which described character in terms of bodily attitudes were uncannily accurate, for instance, the stubborn did tend to be actually stiff-necked, the stoical, those who would not let a word of self-defense escape when they were mocked, did tend to wear their lips stiff (the "stiff upper lip" of everyday English speech). As his experience in this kind of work increased Reich began to think of character in terms of bodily posture. The body held back in it what the individual had not been able to express (to "let out") on crucial occasions in his life. Such holding back fashioned a large part of a person's attitude toward the world. A man carried with him or on him, turned against himself, all the past he had not been able to cope with.

Reich's man, or perhaps more exactly Reich's patient—and it is a real question which leads to the deepest equivocation in his work, whether he could in any meaningful way distinguish between man and patient, a question somehow related to whether he could distinguish between himself and world—amounts to unfulfilled life: he bursts with it. Reich conceives of character, as expressed in attitudes and in rigidity in the body, as what keeps one from living. It is the wall some men always feel between them and life, the window through which Tonio Kroger looked in upon the dance. Reich named it "armour".

As Reich continued to work with patients, he began to understand that the physical and mental defenses or armouring had their own order. As one was dissolved, another unfolded in its stead. For the therapist to achieve something like a coherent cure these defenses had to be attacked in the reverse of the chronological order of their formation, with the most apparent and obvious coming first. For instance, if a patient was obviously anxious to please, Reich would start by pointing that out and waiting to see what came up next.

In his work on the body Reich began to understand that the tensions in the muscles which expressed holding back and corresponded to mental attitudes also had their own coherence. The network of repeated denials and attempts to break through them which made up what Reich called the armour covered and penetrated a person's whole body in ribbon-like segments more or less perpendicular to the spinal chord. He compared the band-like shape of the armour to the segments or rings on a worm, the tightening effect of the armour to the transformation of undulating movement of the worm into the agonized twisting and squirming which occurred when one segment was pressed slightly down with a twig. On the analogy of the worm the human body had a natural expression and a natural response to the world which armouring pinned down and distorted and finally betrayed. On the mental or spiritual plane this armouring betrayed itself in the inability of individuals spontaneously to do and say the right thing, in experiencing what one should do of one's own accord as something one had to do, in having to tell oneself what to say or do instead of simply responding.

Armour kept a person from being himself. It also represented the result of his past struggle with life, with what had threatened his life; but it tended to turn that struggle into a struggle against life. Armour gave an individual a sense of being caged in. It turned his affection to fawning, his love to lust, his anger to spite. If the armour was acute it betrayed the best in a man and turned it into something close to its opposite. Armour turned many people into parodies of what they wished to be and might have become. (Incidentally, in Reich's tendency to obscure the distinction between what a person wished to be and what he might have become lies another of his deepest equivocations.) It was armour that for generations had given men the sense of being excluded from the garden of Eden.

To a large extent individuals are not aware of their armour, certainly in its physical expression. That is, they do not feel the tenseness of their muscles, their holding back. They experience it in a more general way as something which keeps them from themselves, as, for instance, the incapacity to say what they have on their mind in a crucial instance, or generally to mean what they say, or to be moved by a flower or a landscape when they know it to be beautiful.

What were individuals armouring against? In part, and more superficially, they armoured against irrational feelings and impulses, against the anti-social impulses they felt shoot through them. In this sense armour was partly rational, for it saw to restraining what had to be restrained. But why did individuals have to keep themselves from doing things that were obviously irrational, why did it even occur to them to do such things?

Everything pointed to a coherence of the armour, to a general system. There was nothing arbitrary about the armouring, although it received different accents and emphases in different individuals. It seemed to have a general purpose, to mean one thing. Always, in its thousands of manifestations, there seemed to be something consistent about it, something which made it recognizable as the same mechanism no matter what dress it wore. Armour was a denial, in part a necessary denial, but also in part an unnecessary denial; in part, that is, a self-denial. Why did this denial occur? What was being denied?

Reich knew how to wait. In developing his conception of therapy, he had learned to wait to see what would occur next of its own after one defense had been resolved and understood. In some way he always followed nature's lead. At his deepest and simplest Reich was a great reader of nature. Like Michael Faraday he knew how to wait upon it, to let it speak for itself.[3] He did not attempt to force it with highly complicated experiments into giving answers to questions he imposed on it. He let it alone and listened to its dialogue with the world, to the questions it asked and the answers it gave. In this readiness to let things unfold he contrasts sharply with many of his disciples who think their inability to be surprised testifies to their competence.

The questions were, what was at the center of this armour? What was behind it? Reich's readiness to wait meant he knew the answer, if there was any answer, could only come from the armour itself, by following its lead as each layer was dissolved. Its general coherence indicated it had to be leading somewhere.

Following the armour meant pursuing what most people would deny. It meant that the patient could not discover the rational in himself until he faced all the irrational within him. Typically, Reich did not ask himself whether such daring goals did not exceed what one could reasonably expect of professionals.

Although the destructive, even murderous impulses which Reich assumed to lie underneath the surface would clearly be irrational if they broke to the surface, Reich judged them to be distorted reflections of an original, rational anger at humiliating and crippling experiences which the patient as a child had dared not express. The therapy strove gradually to distinguish the murder from this anger, to release the anger and thereby reach the underlying capacity for love. But in order to do this it had to bring out and face all the irrationality in an individual. Its ruling assumption was that an individual without the capacity to express anger—as distinguished from murder—freely and appropriately could not love truly and deeply.

Mostly, as in psychoanalysis, words gave Reich the lead. It was the mixture of violence and sexual obsession in fantasies, expressed verbally, that led him to understand that they had to be disentangled from each other in order slowly to work through to the rational element of anger distorted in the fantasies of violence, and to the rational capacity for love and desire distorted in the perverse and obsessive sexual fantasies. But if words gave Reich the lead, his grasp of the way they were lodged in the body allowed him to find out something about their meaning—to which the words only pointed obliquely.

Working within the framework of psychoanalysis—in fact at this time Reich did not even imagine his work would eventually force him to break with it—Reich understood armour finally as armouring against pleasure, as restricting the capacity for pleasure in work and in love. In this view the misery of individuals was in a certain sense self-inflicted, for it is imposed on the individual by a part of himself, his armour, which lasted much longer than the situation which originally produced it and which tended to reinforce itself, to use life for its reinforcement. In part Reich discovered this incapacity for pleasure in work with German and Austrian youths. In his sexual counseling clinics he noticed many young people were incapable of coping with the sexual freedom he sought to encourage. As he talked to these youths and to his patients he was astonished to discover how many suffered from sexual disturbances when they made love. As he further questioned patients he discovered that if he dropped conventional criteria for potency, which limited themselves to erective potency, and took into account such matters as premature ejaculation and the intensity of pleasure and love experienced, almost everybody he dealt with suffered serious sexual problems.

For many, making love was an unconsciously hostile

act, or a way of humiliating themselves. For instance, many men unconsciously thought of themselves as stabbing with their penis when they made love. Many women experienced making love as a kind of rape, as an expression of hate, disgust, contempt they felt they deserved, as something done to them rather than a free yielding. Almost no one Reich talked to experienced feelings of love when they made love. Reich came to think few if any individuals did not suffer severe disturbances making love—disturbances which occurred because their love was all mixed up with hatred and because, as a result, they experienced their desire and love as antithetical to each other.

Reich's account betrays an elemental distress which eloquently testifies to his total lack of preparation for what he encountered. Like a Columbus he suddenly found himself in front of a sea of suffering and desecration through which the niceties and the in part artificial goodwill of everyday life sought to swim. His determination to bear witness to what he saw at creation, when individuals made love, has all of the courage of the greatest men of knowledge. It brought upon him terrible isolation which intensified the isolation he brought upon himself. But his innocence has something forced about it, something of willful ignorance about it, especially when he speaks of his astonishment at the silent fury of shame that his assertion of what actually occurred when individuals made love brought upon him. How could he pretend not to have expected that?

It was clear that the armour restricted the capacity for pleasure. But it was not entirely clear what pleasure was, and why individuals feared it so much. These questions and others like them led Reich to uncover another major area of study, the orgasm, which as it turned out had a direct relation to his first major work isolating the muscular defenses. Like infantile sexuality, or dreams, the orgasm was a major obvious subject no one had ever attempted to look in the face.

Reich in fact had a genius for looking at the obvious, a genius entirely in the noblest traditions of European science, like Newton's falling bodies and Darwin's pigeons. Reich's sense of the obvious contributed to his remarkable sensitivity to evasiveness—the evasiveness of others.[4] It also gave his research a sweep and energy and a confidence which is stirring. Like few researchers he had a sense of the important, of the uncanny resemblances between disparate phenomena. In attempting to overcome the embarrassment before the obvious of many individuals, including himself, Reich used to repeat Goethe's beautiful poem, "Do you know what is hardest, what you think is easiest, to see what lies before your eyes."

Reich attempted to understand orgasm by studying its purpose. In classical experiments (which as far as I know have not been repeated) Reich noticed that there was a significant difference in the electrical charge of the skin of individuals when they were merely mechanically excited, say by a feather or pornographic pictures, and when they were moved or excited by a person they made love to.[5] That is that there was a difference in kind between masturbation and love.

Rudimentary as they were, these experiments appeared to confirm the distinction he had begun to make in his clinical work between mechanical or erective potency and the capacity to experience pleasure, which he was later to call orgastic potency. Although crudely and faintly, the experiments pointed to a difference in quality of experience when people made love which was determined by whether they loved. By experimentally pointing to differences in intensities of life, Reich came close to discovering values in nature, for he was showing experimentally that at one moment one person was *more* alive than another.

Reich had much difficulty in dealing with the implications of his discovery of values in nature. He thought the discovery of values in nature absolved man from thinking. The discovery of values in nature appeared to confirm him in his feeling that man's thought was superfluous at best, at worst a ready instrument of subterfuge, for convincing people of what they knew was not so. In fact he came quite close to thinking that thought represented not much more than a fear of nature and her values, that thought was merely artificial and finally evasive.

In the actual study of the orgasm, Reich tried to distinguish between undisturbed and disturbed orgasms, in his thought, armoured and unarmoured. The distinction was drawn in part relatively but also finally in kind, in terms of pleasure and satisfaction and well-being. For in heavily armoured individuals orgasm gave hardly any satisfaction, and in fact occurred prematurely, or in any case without satisfaction, because they feared pleasure. He saw the function of the orgasm as the discharge of energy or emotion (at this point energy meant for him nothing much different from Freud's *libido*, that is something one thought existed but had not experienced—except in thought). Pleasure, he began to understand, occurred in direct proportion to the extent an individual could yield to himself, his partner and nature. In other words orgasm represented something close to the turning point of most armour, that is, what many individuals dreaded most, and which they spent a great deal of their life's time defending against and at the same time almost vindictively yearning for.

By yielding Reich meant something specific as well as general. He meant the ability of an individual to let go at the climax, to experience involuntary movements of his body and thought.

At the climax of orgasm the individual no longer told his body what to do but listened to it, he let go of himself, so that his body as well as his feelings moved of their own, softly, like waves. The hands and thoughts and pelvis all seem to move of themselves. Reich compared these involuntary movements (which could only occur in an individual relatively unarmoured) to the contractions and expansions of an amoeba. In fact he thought the movements of orgasm betrayed in the highly differentiated human being his basic relation to the amoeba. It was in part because man experienced this kinship with the animals and the lowly worm and amoeba when he made love that for centuries he had been held in the grip of such contradictory feelings towards love, both ascetic and pornographic, which had brought him into deep conflict with himself and made him, often, a victim of the best in himself. This was the meaning of the crucifixion: that he would destroy the best in himself—but not forget it.

The most important point in his description of the climax is the conception of involuntary movements and emotions in which the individual becomes nothing more than pulsating protoplasm, as Reich once described it. It provided Reich with the key to his understanding of nature—to his sense that nature could take care of itself if man did not impede it and try to dominate it, to his sense that man *could* be spontaneously rational, if his impulses to rationality, which were inextricably connected with his impulses to genitality, were not thwarted.

For him all intellectual and artistic creation depended on an individual's readiness to yield to nature and himself. Unless you let go, he kept telling his patient Myron Sharaf, you will never do anything.[6] The main fear of human beings was of letting go, of everything that occurred of its own, and although this fear was often justified because underneath the surface lurked all sorts of irrationality, at its deepest it represented a fear of the involuntary movements of love. Reich was talking in concrete terms of what Goethe's Egmont meant when he remarked that the best things in life come unasked. One could not live with pleasure, that is, have the sensation one was actually living, rather than the memory of having lived, unless one could yield to the involuntary, that is, unless one did not defend against life.

As he began to understand what nature meant in orgasm, Reich tried also to understand why fear of the involuntary gripped individuals. The inability to give in to involuntary feelings and movements when making love he called orgastic impotence. He considered it almost endemic.

In his patients, when treatment progressed and when they were approaching health, he began to expect symptoms of orgasm anxiety, for instance, dreams of falling or fears of coming apart. The involuntary movements of orgasm and their pleasure represented the quick of life—not for nothing were the genitals the centers of creation. They also represented the core of what the organism armoured against, in a sense life itself. That was what, for one reason or another, individuals really feared or had been made to fear.

As the many outer layers of armour gradually loosened, the central disturbance and fear close to the core would arise, the fear of giving in—to oneself, another, and the world. This yielding was perceived as disintegration or death. At this point in treatment patients who had previously gloried themselves in their potency often became temporarily impotent. Rather than as a symptom of sickness, Reich came to consider this temporary impotence an important indication of health, of the resumption of some dialogue between emotion and the body. It indicated that an individual had ceased to hang on to his erective potency as a badge of his virility. It meant that penis and body had again become soft and responsive to the emotions instead of their masters. That a man allowed himself to become excited instead of telling himself to be excited, allowed love to stir of its own instead of provoking it. In short it meant a person would again surprise himself, that he could distinguish between what he actually felt, what he wanted himself, and what he felt others expected him to feel. In a sense he now could become his own man because he dared to allow himself to become a bit of nature. This coming apart of what was held together by force so that it could cohere of itself was perhaps what Crazy Jane dimly sensed, 'For nothing can be sole or whole/That has not been rent.' But Reich had little respect for poets.

At the same time, and because the concept of orgastic potency showed the purpose and, therefore, the coherence of armour, it allowed Reich to set a clear therapeutic goal: the restoration of orgastic potency. He assumed (I think it is really no more than that) that the effects of the restoration of orgastic potency (which, it should be remembered, could not occur without carefully undoing and understanding the whole irrational side of a person's character) represented mental and emotional health, or at least put an individual in a position where he had the strength to live in a rational manner if he chose.

Reich's work on the orgasm played an important part in bringing him into conflict with Freud, one of the most crucial struggles in Reich's turbulent life. We know it only from Reich's account.[7] Although Freud acknowledged to Reich that if he was right he would be his true heir and would have eventually to shoulder the burden of the truths of psychoanalysis, Freud could not bring himself to accept Reich's work on the orgasm. After much hesitation the psychoanalytic publishing house refused to publish *Character Analysis*. In part Freud suspected Reich because of his political activities. Freud entertained no illusions about what it meant to be a member of the Communist Party; he pointed out to Reich that it compromised his intellectual independence just as much as membership in the S.J. would have. But the conflict was deeper than that.

More than any other student of Freud's, Reich imitated his method rather than repeated his conclusions. Reich's work on the orgasm recalled Freud's earlier work on infantile sexuality and the crippling effects of sexual repression just at a time when Freud, with his fashioning of the death instinct, was in effect repudiating its implications. With his fresh insistence on the relation between capacity for pleasure and freedom from neurosis, Reich must have brought home to Freud in intolerable fashion the implicit contradictions between the work of his prime, which affirmed pleasure, and the work of his old age, which argued man also wished to suffer.

Although painful, the conflict between Freud and Reich appears to have unfolded in a straightforward and honorable enough manner to allow each man to continue to respect the other. I am tempted to call it the last of the struggles of the old school in which one adversary respected the other rather than desired his annihilation. Such kind of respect indicates each antagonist is likely to be in part right.

In contrast to Freud, who tended to conceive of character as divided between conscious and unconscious, Reich saw it as made up of three layers, conscious, unconscious and core. In Reich's view the conscious, that is the polite everyday behavior, represented a kind of forced parody of the core. Ideals, manners, etc. dimly reflected what individuals were in their core, but were prevented from becoming by their armour. It was the slow burn of those imprisoned aspirations that provoked much desperate, even violent public and private behavior.

Perhaps the earliest presentation of Reich's view occurred in his classic refutation of Freud's death instinct in *Character Analysis*. Where Freud posited a primary masochism, Reich understood masochism as a secondary reaction, a yearning to have the armour, the wall which kept the individual from life, pierced. The tragedy was that the piercing involved pain and even death (as in *hara-kiri*); yet it was not pain and death the individual yearned for, but relief, relief from what kept him from living the life he felt in him. Where Freud's view pointed to the necessity of restraint, Reich's tended to point to the possibility of a world that would act rationally without having to force itself to it. Reich's deep confidence in self-regulation in all aspects of life sprang from his experience of the self-regulation of the involuntary movements of both heart and body in love.

Energy

It was as consequence of Reich's understanding of the pattern of armour and its segmental arrangement and of the function of orgasm in the formation of character that the most crucial and the most difficult to cope with, and at the same time the simplest, most obvious, most questionable, most notorious of his discoveries occurred. Almost from the moment he had begun to deal more actively with patients, Reich had been aware of the physical reactions which accompanied understanding when it occurred with affect. As patients improved they described feelings of pleasure at the edge of the skin, waves of pleasure moving through them, a sense of sweetness in their limbs, as well as soft sensations of pulsation in their pelvis. Always scrupulously respectful of the accuracy of the metaphors of everyday speech, Reich took these descriptions seriously and let them work on him.

Why was it that when the spasms of the muscles were gradually released the patients felt warmth flowing in them, that their skin appeared flushed and grew tanned, that as their defenses loosened they felt a sweetness rippling through them? What was desire, how did a person feel desire, why did he feel it toward one person and not to another? What occurred in orgasm that gave satisfaction, what did it mean to talk of the discharge of energy or libido?

Reich began to think in terms of an actual energy which existed within and outside of individuals. In doing this Reich took another metaphor literally. Freud had always spoken of *libido* in perhaps metaphorical terms, or at least in metaphysical terms. That is he had spoken of it as if it existed and we all knew it existed, if only because we understood what he meant when he talked of it, but had never claimed he could show it visibly and measurably in nature. He had spoken of it as if we could perceive it with our thought but not our eyes.

As Reich began to uncover the dialogue between body and soul, between words, past memories, affect and bodily posture, he began to wonder if the descriptions of the sensations of his patients might be literally true, if some energy might not actually be streaming through them when they described sensations of sweetness and waves. At the same time he noticed, in some work he was doing on the disintegration of matter (meat and grass), that a blue glow formed about it and that his hands especially tended to grow slightly tanned from working with such matter.[8] Slowly, Reich began to connect this blue light with the hypothesis of an energy which corresponded to Freud's libido. It was literally the glow of life itself. It was what made up the blue of the sky and could be seen with the naked eye about the human body, especially about the genitals and head, for instance surrounding the heads of actors on stage. (The halo about the head of Christian paintings probably reflects some memory of perception of this energy.) To test the objection that his perceptions were subjective, Reich exposed photographic plates to this energy. Lately, work in the Soviet Union which establishes body fields of energy appears to confirm some of his work, independently of his understanding of its significance.[9] The discovery of this energy led Reich to a theory of the formation of matter. Experiments which showed extremely high reactions on a Geiger counter when radium was brought into contact with concentrations of orgone energy also led Reich to postulate a relationship between orgone energy and nuclear energy.[10] He thought of orgone energy as the energy which came before matter, and radioactive as that which came after matter. It was the build up of orgone energy which made for desire in the human organism and which was discharged in orgasm. Except for showing that higher concentrations of energy drew energy to them, thus explaining how the human organism drew energy from the surrounding atmosphere, Reich significantly did not really deal with why it was two orgone energy fields (two human beings) experienced attraction to each other. He acknowledged his inability to cope with the problem when, in a somewhat different context, he stated that he could not make sense of the differentiation of the sexes.

The discovery of orgone energy is the most dramatic

and most questionable moment in Reich's work. It marks the transition from dealing with specific individuals to dealing with the nature of life itself. He called it, I think quite rightly, the discovery of the living. I have given it here cursory and inadequate treatment, partly because I do not have the scientific training to evaluate Reich's experiments.

Except for a few remarks, I shall not deal with Reich's later work, the work which grew from his work on energy. Because I have no experimental experience of it, I would not be able to do much except repeat Reich's explanations and reasons for them. In it, however, Reich fell prey to a reductionism which amounts to a kind of natural determinism. Everything in this work is seen in terms of energy functions, blocked or unblocked energy functions. It leaves no place for thought or consciousness. There is a distrust of words and language which is very strange. For Reich was a splendid child of Europe's love of rationality, perhaps her last, if one can speak of her at all in her present divided and shrunken state.

Of the rest of Reich's experimental research most startling, perhaps, is Reich's work on cancer. While in no sense claiming he had a cure for cancer, Reich did elaborate a coherent view of the relation of character to the predisposition to cancer and of the somatic and biological expression of this relation. Cancer represented an anticipation and to a certain extent a parody of the natural process of dying, of gradual withdrawal from life. Individuals who in some basic way shrank from life, who were overcome by their dread of it were predisposed to cancer.

As in all of Reich's work, expressions, such as "shrinking from life," which are most often allowed truth only when they are used in a metaphorical sense, were taken literally and shown to have biological significance. The neglect of Reich's coherent picture of the disease is puzzling when one reflects that some cancer research points in fragmented way to Reich's understanding of the disease.

Politics

During the time of his work on armour and orgasm Reich attempted to relate his findings to the political situation about him, first in Vienna from 1927 until 1930 and then in Berlin from 1930 to 1933. During this time he wrote several remarkable works on irrationality in politics (he thought of it as the irrationality of politics): *The Sexual Revolution* (second German language edition, 1935), *The Mass Psychology of Fascism* (first German language edition, 1933), and *People in Trouble* (written during the period 1927-45, published in English, 1953). Reich wanted to understand the relation between private and public crisis. And he wanted to act in society on his understanding, much in the way he acted on his patients.

Reich's involvement in politics, especially his readiness to join the Communist party (1927-1932) and to disregard the distinction between professional and civil activity, is the most crucial in his life.[11] All the more crucial because Reich was not aware and never became aware of what this involvement did to him.

In his work on, and in his participation in, irrational politics, Reich tried to answer the question of why men put up with their own oppression. No tyranny on earth, he reasoned, could last for any length of time if a great many people did not in some manner accept it. Why were many (Reich typically thought, all) people unable to say "no" to their oppressors and mean it?

Reich's answer to this question represents an attempt to apply what he had discovered about the incapacity of many individuals to experience pleasure to political life. The inability to act courageously and effectively in situations which threatened life, and submissiveness in general, occurred because individuals no longer dared rely on themselves, on what they saw stirring before their eyes and felt moving within their breasts—and in their brains. The mechanism for crushing confidence (that is a living relation to what one was) consisted, most importantly, in crippling the emotional life through enforced chastity. The main mechanism for doing this was what Reich called the compulsive family. Enforced chastity from adolescence to the time of marriage reinforced the Oedipus complex, making sons and daughters incapable of rationally defying their parents and looking out for themselves.

In Reich's view the capacity of adolescent men and women to love each other indicated that their emotional energy was no longer trapped in the aspect of their relationship to their parents, which was made up of fantasy. Effective suppression of relationships between adolescents reinforced the Oedipus complex and made for an inability to experience pleasure and feeling. It tended to shape individuals for whom making love and feeling, especially loving, were in some sense antithetical. When such individuals grew older and got what they wanted, they were for the most part incapable of enjoying it, of feeling love. They had become so disassociated from their inner self that they experienced their desire pornographically, mixed up with feelings of contempt, self-disgust and hatred. Because over long years individuals had been compelled to overcome themselves, they were no longer capable of recognizing when their independence was threatened and fighting back. They were divided against themselves.

In Reich's view Fascism and Nazism exploited this division of individuals against themselves. They exploited, for instance, the conflict between the yearning of young people for love relationships and their fear and resentment of their parents. He saw, for instance, how the Nazis, through their youth organizations, gave young people the illusion of freedom from their families—only to imprison them in the party and in fanatical loyalty to a leader. He thought that only genuine relationships with their peers would free them from the resort to mystical solutions of their conflicts.

With great daring and perhaps some foolhardiness Reich attempted to deal with the problems of young people in concrete fashion. He held meetings under the sponsorship of the Communist party in which he attempted to deal in a matter-of-fact manner with the conflicts young people felt between their yearning for partners and their entanglement with their families. In contrast to the usual Communist political meetings these meetings of Reich's stirred deep response. A response which baffled the rigid Communist party hierarchy, who could not conceive of a relation between private life, especially enforced chastity, and the incapacity to defy oppression.

But Reich's readiness to entertain easy expectations did not blind him to their disappointment. He recognized his failures. He was, however, unaware of the extent of his inability to cope with them. As a result of his political and clinical work in Vienna and Berlin, where he attempted to support relationships between young people, Reich faced up to the incapacity of many individuals to cope with sexual freedom in a rational manner, that is without abusing it. He learned that changed conditions did not change individuals immediately. That is, "sexual freedom" would not "cure," of itself and immediately, the submissiveness which came of asceticism. He explained this incapacity, however, perhaps too easily, in terms of their earlier upbringing which made people incapable of coping with what they yearned for. To expose such individuals to sexual freedom amounted, in his later view, to teasing them with it and bringing their impotence home to them. For there was nothing more likely to bring home an individual's self-disgust and weakness than sexual activity without affect. He hated most of all the abuse of the freedoms he desired to support. But the fact is that it is extremely difficult in matters of love to tell abuse from freedom. In his later years Reich came to think that too rapid pushes towards an apparently ideal freedom, especially in the political sphere, actually undermined the freedom they tried to bring about.

Reich's realization that changed conditions did not change character, that in fact they tended to drive men into irrational behaviour by facing them with a freedom with which they could not cope, provided the theoretical reason for his break with Marxism and Communism and incidentally, the basic insight for his understanding of the failure of the Soviet Revolution *(The Sexual Revolution,* 1935). After his break with the Communist party Reich still continued to take oppressors for granted in an astonishingly casual manner. He thought, however, it made little sense to attack oppressors before individuals had dealt with their own internalization of oppression.

There is in this final attitude much resignation, for it implies all political action is futile. In some sense this resignation is also implicit in the revolutionary ideology which preceded it. For seizure of power by force implies individuals cannot help themselves without hurting others, that is that strength can only come from the weakness of others.

EXPERIENCE

Therapy

I do not pretend to understand Reichian therapy entirely, but I do not think the professional explanations account for it. In fact my real bother with them is that they will tolerate no doubt, that they are final about matters in which a wise man would be cautious, and that they make exaggerated claims. They claim to explain everything. As a young man when I first grew interested in Reich's work I was fascinated (and thought I was impressed) by such absolute claims, claims that would admit of no doubt. I took them for assurance. I wanted the answers and I wanted them in a hurry. Now ... well, now the difference between facts, and something one wishes, one wants, one knows has to be true impresses me.

Reichian therapy is characterized by harsh, grueling

criticism of the patient. The therapist is quick to point out arrogance, conceit, insincerity (as revealed in tone of voice), righteousness, servility, overreadiness to please. At first the criticism applies only to surface characteristics, what any perceptive observer might see and usually in social situations seeks to ignore. As the therapy deepens, the criticism grows more telling and at the same time less harsh to the patient's vanity. For by that time he has been made to drop the petty resorts of conceit and inflated self-esteem.

Depending on the character of the patient the therapist will point to his inability to get angry in appropriate situations, to his contempt, to his tendency to take flight into passive homosexuality (for instance, by taking on seductive airs with the therapist), because he fears to stand up and fight. The patient accepts this criticism, because it strikes home and it quickens him, as home truths when they are disinterested always quicken one.

During this harsh attack the patient lies flat with his legs drawn up on a bed, naked, except for underwear. The therapist sits near him. Although the patient can look the therapist in the face, because he is lying down and is close to totally exposed, he is to a certain extent disarmed and does not readily react in his usual manner. It is thought that somehow by accepting a defenceless and vulnerable posture the patient will more readily betray what he really feels and allow himself to be unmasked. The therapy is a passion of unmasking —as was Reich's life.

In itself the assumption of the therapy that vulnerability reveals something essential is curious, for it presupposes that a person will reveal his true character in a situation that would embarrass anybody. The patients, in my experience, do not experience this vulnerability as in some sense appropriate to the situation, but experience it rather as proof of their own weakness.

Perhaps the real question is why any individual puts himself in such a situation. What brings individuals to expose themselves in this fashion, to treat their souls as impersonally as their bodies in a doctor's office, as if they were objects to be moved about on an examination table? I do not think it is desperation, not a desperation at any rate that knows itself as such, or at least not simply desperation, but desperation mixed up with exaltation. It is a desperation full of conceit and vanity, for it deems that the greatest weakness somehow entitles one to become the best.

In this mixture of desperation and exaltation the patients reflect Reich's own rough sternness and soaring expectation. Throughout his writings until his last years resilient confidence follows upon harshest criticism.

In part it is Reich's assurances of what will come that sets the patient's determination to endure almost anything for the sake of change. There is, however, something cheap about this courage. Patients are ready to take real chances with their lives, greater risks than probably most of them realize, but only with absolute guarantees of success, guarantees which Reich was surprisingly ready to give. This desperate desire for change of the patients bears some resemblance to the revolutionary yearning that has made such havoc of this century. Like it, it wants change without taking responsibility for it. The patients want change done to them, like an operation almost, an operation to their mind and soul, their being—not their body. As a result, there is a large element of flight in this readiness for change, which itself probably springs from a dim foreboding of being incapable of growth. It is marked by impatience.

People also put up with this therapy because they seek relief from the endemic flattery in much of our lives, in educational institutions where teachers "encourage" students because they are afraid to criticize, in movies, novels, in much of what passes for "art", in advertising. In short this therapy appeals to people who wish to be honest with themselves but do not have the strength of heart to do it of themselves and so want it done to them, want, that is, to be relieved of the risks of error or misjudgment. Incidentally, it tells something about our letters, our literature, our "philosophy", that one cannot look to it but must look to a therapist for aid in self-knowledge, for commonsense.

Behind the therapy's harsh criticism lies the conviction that the patients will not take the chance of standing on their own two feet before the neurotic crutches are knocked out from under them. When the therapist is in good faith, that is, when he puts the patient's welfare above his devotion to Reich's truth, such criticism will nurture the best in one, the courage to learn, etc. It also, perhaps more importantly and more questionably, lends the patient moral assurance, a quality now feared as much as it is yearned for among "sophisticated" people. For it somehow represents the inner voice one hears but dares not listen to—the inner voice that makes for the growth of the world, or its destruction.

At the same time that the therapists crush oblique defiance, that is, defiance that testifies to impotence, for instance, in backbiting or contempt, they encourage defiance in areas where it is hardest, toward parents and wives and husbands and lovers. The therapist tends to assume that the anger young men and women spite upon their universities or upon themselves would break out in straightforward and, therefore revivifying manner, if the patients directed it against its true object, their parents. In the therapists' view the patients pick on the educational institutions, and the society in general, because it takes less courage to defy them than to stand up to one's parents. (In an important recent book, *The Age of Sensation,* Robert Hendin has also pointed to the considerable amount of suppressed and repressed rage toward parents among disaffected youths.) In their attempt to redirect the anger of their patients toward its proper object, the therapists work on the (in my judgment correct) principle that emotion expressed on a substitute object cannot find relief, because it does not know itself for what it is.

In their interference in relationships of love the therapists are more dogmatic and programmatically insistent than in anything else. They assume from the start that any relationships fashioned before therapy are largely irrational. In many instances, the break-up of marriages and love-affairs tends to come close to the proof of progress in therapy. The assumption here, again correct in my judgment, is that it is better to go it alone, to give oneself a chance to start again, than to clutch on to a bad and twisted relationship as if it were for dear life.

The bother is that the therapists come perilously close to thinking that it is impossible for rational relationships to grow in the world beyond their purview. [arrogant] Reich wrote pessimistically about the life of genuine love among individuals who had not been through therapy. In a statement of hateful arrogance Elsworth Baker, a disciple of Reich's, feels called upon to state that most of what is called love among the untreated (for which one should probably read at least in part, uninitiated) springs from fear and hatred.[12] The trouble with such statements on the part of Reich's disciples is that they grow not from experience of life, which could not but make one more cautious and respectful, but from Reich's authority, and from what at its worst and most desperate amounted to Reich's necessity to deny the validity of other people's lives. The disciples hold such judgments to be true because Reich made them, not because they have seen what they testify to with their own eyes. That is something of what is wrong.

There is also a deeper problem with the therapy, which is, however, in some way related to the programmatic convictions of the therapist. I mean that a third party's decisive interference with the relations between children and parents, and between lovers, can never be unambiguous. By decisive interference I mean that the therapists do not shirk from confronting a patient with a choice between his own health and emotional growth and a relationship he had previously assumed to be at the center of his life. This often amounts to choosing between continuing therapy and other centers of his or her life. The breaks that are thus brought about are deep, perhaps the deepest individuals can endure. The rub is that inevitably they are brought about on the authority of somebody else, on the authority of a therapist who himself tends to adhere, often slavishly, to Reich's teachings.

It is no easy matter to get into contact with feelings of anger toward parents—and there is something deeply wrong with substituting a therapist's opinion that one should be angry with one's parents for the actual experience of those feelings. I am saying that in some real sense the therapy represents a violation of consciousness of an individual for the sake of a theory. I do not know how many individuals could go through such a break on their own. To undergo it on another's authority may amount only to transferring one's fear and subservience to one's parents, if it is that, to another individual and ultimately to Reich's teachings.

In Reich's instance the break with parents which is so characteristic of his therapy was in a sense forced on him by life, as I shall explain at the end of this essay. It is not clear to what extent he came to terms with it in himself. Until that is clear one has to ask to what extent he felt compelled to force such a break with parents on others, because he had not come to terms with it in his own life.

The patient submits to the therapist's judgment, because he thinks it is completely aboveboard and disinterested. That is a very big assumption, and I have my doubts whether it is warranted, whether it is a compliment to any human being to trust him so implicitly. The corresponding insistence on the perfection and the absoluteness of the theory, and, by implication, of the therapists in Reichian circles masks terror, insecurity, at times even hatred. One does individuals and their theories the greatest compliment when one sees their limitation. In limitless idolatry there is always some drive to self-immolation, to renouncing all responsibility for one's own life.

Although Reich desired to resolve the relationship between therapist and patient, to render it completely aboveboard, I think his work and life actually shows how ambiguous and complicated it is and how difficult if not impossible a task it is to resolve it. I do not know if it is possible to "allow" the sort of independence he thought he wished of his patients. Used in this sense the very word "allow" comes close to meaning manipulate. In many instances I know of individuals involved in Reichian therapy, it has led to an independence, which though at times it feels free, is unpredictable without being arbitrary, almost always has in its background a fierce and rigid adherence to Reich's literal words.

There is always something uncanny and frightening about it, something cold, a refusal to see what is obvious and before the eyes, a refusal, I think, to see anything that Reich did not state. There is also almost always an adoration for Reich bordering on idolatry. In the end Reich fled the society of men, because he could not come to terms with his relationship to his patients. All his attempts to resolve it only deepened his experience of its ambiguity.

In my experience, which is limited—I have taken no surveys—Reichian patients have had very difficult family situations, what are called by professionals "traumatic family situations." (Again, it is important to note that Robert Hendin thinks such situations are much more common than one would readily assume.) They are often patients who are in some sense fatherless. As Paul Goodman once said, there is something unearthly about the fatherless. But the unearthly, one should remember, are not necessarily the divine.

They are also patients who cannot conceive of family relations as in any sense rational or natural. As a result they have the unshakeable sense that they are living in a dream, a dream perhaps not unlike the dream of Descartes or the dream of the knight of the sorrowful countenance. It is that dream they want to wake up from, but do not dare wake themselves up from. The therapy can help them wake from this dream; can bring them, that is, to feel whatever hatred they feel for their parents. It can make them taste the freedom of orphans, sorrowful as it is.

In doing this it can bring them to the point where they can actually experience the love they feel for their parents—something, if I am not mistaken, Reich hardly imagined as a result of his therapy. If it does not bring a patient to the point (which is not its conscious goal) where he can see his parents for what they are, which amounts to loving them, the therapy runs the serious risk of waking the patient from one dream to enchant him with another. This second dream is a collective dream, it has its own language, it is the dream of Reich from which tragedy only may have perhaps awakened him, it is no less a dream because it reflects a *part* of the truth. In fact it has become a dream and not simply a part of the truth, because Reich insisted it was *all* the truth, which really amounted to saying he had discovered certain things, because he feared to know others. I mean he used his truth to shield him from other truths.

For if Reich taught that we were all children of nature it is also true that we would not be alive unless we were the sons and daughters of specific parents, who loved each other as best they could, which is an historical occurrence, unique, full of obvious flaws, without which glory, the glory Reich so yearned for and despised, is not possible.

The roughness of the therapy is matched by its overprotectiveness. Perhaps, more than in other forms of therapy, the patients tend to stay in it far too long, making of it something of a substitute for living itself. For who among those who drove themselves out of Eden can say anybody is healthy enough for Eden? Baker's repeated odd remarks that in life one has to take risks betray this overprotectiveness, which complements a ruthless interference in private life—an interference which runs the real risk of provoking a dependence on the therapy and Reich's *ipsissima verba* no less cloying than the one the patient wishes to grow out of.[13] Shouldn't it be obvious, if one lives at all, that one has to make one's own mistakes?

Within these critical limitations the therapy, in the hands of a skillful therapist, can achieve remarkable results. I qualify "in the hands of a skillful therapist," because as perhaps in all medicine and in fact in all knowing the man is more important than the learning, although only the learning allows the man to become what he is. Instead in Reichian circles an alarming, obtuse fixation on Reich's technique tends to prevail, which shields the patients from looking at the therapists, the therapists from looking at themselves.

I mean by remarkable achievements, that the therapy helps people. It restores their capacity for work, their capacity to love their work and to find work worthy of love, to love what they touch and their capacity not to touch what they do not love, to live in the here-and-now and not in the expectation of the future or in regret for the past. (In this last instance the therapy in fact suffers from the defect of its virtue, for it tends to blunt foresight.) The therapy knows how to call on the resources in people, how to let them reach their own strength. It helps them grow into men who respect what is worthy of respect and hate what is worthy of hate and not, as so often is the case (for how else finally to explain the spread of the slave states throughout the world?), who hate what is worthy of respect and who submit to what is worthy of hate in ascetic self-rejection. But as I have indicated there is a price or at least a risk in this therapy. All too often the improvement brings with it a mystical, literal-minded devotion to Reich and his work—an adherence which at its worst will not let one word or thought stir of its own, as if what Reich had not explained is not worthy of explanation. In such attitudes there is much hatred and resentment.

In other words the therapy creates almost as many problems as it resolves. These new problems, which are probably not as severe as the problems the patients come to therapy with, cannot be coped with, however, unless the patients have the courage to go beyond the world-view of the therapy. Just this is the hardest step of all, for it means acknowledging and experiencing the limitations of the therapy, which are also the limitations of Reich's character.

The tendency among Reichians, however, is to do just the opposite, to do everything on Reich's authority. This tendency among Reichians to do everything on Reich's authority, even though he is long dead, strives in some sense to perpetuate Reich's surprising readiness when he was alive to assume responsibility for almost everything, especially for what an individual must take responsibility for himself. I mean he invited many to use his name—and grew furious when they abused it. In an important sense he never distinguished himself from his therapy, his work from his character.

In an oblique manner in his work on what he called the "Emotional Plague" and in his late work on Christ and saviors he touched on the problem of his own relationship to his own work and attempted to come to some kind of symbolic understanding of it. But somehow he never really looked it fully in the face. Even at the last he could argue he was simply a natural scientist.

I think his last struggle, the terrible struggle with the

Food and Drug Administration, brought this problem of his understanding of himself in deepest focus, deeper focus than he could withstand. The government called upon him to defend himself and his work. But Reich ran at the time of the prosecution. He ran by defying but not fighting.[14] I think he did this because he could not face himself and distinguish himself from his work.

In some sense Reich understood others so well, rather what kept others from being themselves so well, because he was evading himself also. In this sense he realized himself in the lives of others instead of in his own. Is this what a doctor should do in order to cure?

(Ultimately and daily one has to live one's own life as well as the life of nature.) Reich wanted to live the life of nature, because he feared his own life. But surely one cannot live nature's life unless one lives one's own.

How much of what he said to others could he have said to himself? Would he have listened to others address him in the ruthless manner he addressed his patients? It is because of his own inability in some sense to accept himself that the acceptance of his work by the outside world (and somehow with Reich there was always an outside and an inside world) became crucial, a question in the end literally of life and death, for Reich died at the legal rejection of his work: he saw many of his books almost literally burned before his eyes.

I think this inability to distinguish his character from his work helps to explain his tendency to view the character of others as almost exclusively irrational. His assurance that the self of others was irrational kept him from facing his own self and grasping its limitations. In fact if Reich feared anything it was limitations. He could not distinguish them from arbitrary restraints.

As a result of Reich's inability to distinguish himself from his work, the role of Reichian therapists, despite all Reich's effort to understand it, cannot be distinguished from a defense of, even a recreation of his character. When Reichian therapists refer to Reich's authority in justifying their actions, they also in some sense imagine themselves to be reincarnating his person. It is this inability to distinguish themselves from him which constantly threatens to turn them into little more than bigoted sectarians.

In short I am saying the therapy works—but I am also asking at what price or perhaps more accurately in what context—in the context of the living world or of enchantment? This is the real question. In a sense it has always been the only question about all of psychoanalysis. Does it somehow rob the individual of his independence, render him afraid of making mistakes, trap him in its own formulations?

On a much cruder level, Reich's discoveries lend themselves to one terrible distortion, a distortion to which probably anyone who deals with them is to some degree heir. They tend to encourage the superstition that there is a shortcut to solving these problems, that one can approach the body and thereby bypass the mind and the heart, that is the painful knowledge of what one is, was and might become, which must occur in words. Extreme and despicable distortions of this kind can be seen in Alexander Lowen's work and in Orson Bean's book.[15] To them the therapy is little more than gymnastics.

In some sense this atittude of gymnastic reductionism is inherent in Reich. Although Reich was fully aware that nothing resembling healing could occur without words and understanding, he was also mighty suspicious of words. In some way he feared them, perhaps especially what somebody might involuntarily ask him. In this sense, in the sense that it allowed him not to talk to the patient face to face, Reich's approach to the body always had something evasive about it, precisely because it could not distinguish between an amoeba and a man, because it protected Reich from what an individual might say back. It is almost as if there was something he could not hear, he would not hear. As he put it, he hated chatter—but I suspect he also feared involuntary reason as distinguished from involuntary fantasy and feeling.

In some way Reich made genitality (orgastic potency) predominate over rationality. This is true even of his conviction that genitality rendered people capable of acting rationally of their own accord. It was as if he wanted to deny the mind's corrective powers and get along without foresight.

I think Reich actually feared the independence of thought and the cold and unexpected light it might throw on his work. In some way he wished to subordinate rationality to genitality in just the way the previous tradition had in large part attempted to subordinate genitality to rationality. For instance the description of the predominance of rationality in the *Republic* of Plato (474 A) could, with the change of few terms, just as well be a description of what Reich meant by genitality and genital primacy. I think Reich's fear of the intellect has something to do with his reluctance to engage in dialogue, to talk to his peers or for that matter his patients.

Reich was acute in his criticism of the misuses of intellect, of the fantasies and brooding many try to convince themselve and others are actual thought. He was ferocious, at times vicious in his criticism of bright people, saying, for instance, that they made love with their heads and thought with their genitals. By which I think he meant a great deal of intellectual work was sexually obsessed and a great deal of love intellectually obsessed, that many men did not make love when they made love, or think when they thought, but instead alternately brooded and masturbated.

But at times Reich also spoke with unpardonable contempt and even a strange bitterness of "culture" and of the great achievements of the past, dismissing, for instance, great philosophical works as of no great importance in comparison to the constipation of millions. In his scorn for culture, he was as usual acutely sensitive to the hypocritical relation many maintained toward it. But there was also in his attitude toward "culture" a strange streak of envy, a strange sense of being left out of it without any accompanying sense that he was largely responsible for this exclusion, because he could not bring himself to admit to himself he was not the first man.

At his best I think Reich desired to distinguish thought from feeling and genitality so that neither could be made covertly to serve the purposes of the other. But his criticism of the intellect frequently exceeded mere well-intentioned harshness. The anti-intellectual purposes his work is often made to serve, for instance, the substitution of feeling for thought, a slogan and dogma which has made such progress in ruining educational institutions including high schools, does not amount to mere distortion. Reich was uneasy with the intellect. He felt about it much the way Huck Finn felt about clean clothes.

Reich's suspicion of the intellect is in some way related to his inability to live with the realization that men thought their own thoughts, made their choices and their mistakes, that many of them, perhaps most of them, would listen to themselves more than to him, and that this was freedom. He would not forgive them for this individuality even as he admired them for it.

Reich's work represents as much an outcry against this individuality which takes its own measure in its self-respect as it is an outcry against irrationality in social and individual life. I mean the individuality which knows, as Irving Kristol profoundly put it, that it lives not in *the* world but in *a* world.

I wonder simply whether the attempt to free others, even when it is done in good faith, as in the instance of Reich, can lead to anything but a covert form of domination. In some way Reich realized this, of course. He reasoned, however, that the only way to blunt the attraction of the parody of total freedom which has wreaked such murder in this century was by being free for real. But I do not know if he really knew any more about how to do that than the best of us, although he thought he did. I fear that his freedom, especially in other hands and minds than his, will turn out to be another enslaving promise, perhaps even more cruel than any that preceded it. The point about freedom is that you cannot give it to anybody. You can only take it away.

It is significant that as far as I know there has been no serious questioning among those who know Reich's work of Reich's assumption that the restoration of orgastic potency would make individuals more effective in other areas.

The simple question that has to be asked here is whether this is so, whether in fact all the consequences which Reich assumed (and I should like to repeat that I think he merely assumed them) flowed from the restoration of orgastic potency. Could it be that the remarkable achievement of restoring some capacity for pleasure and love in an individual did not necessarily make him less neurotic and more rational in other areas? At least these questions should have been raised. It is also significant that no attempt has been made to study former patients to see if they are actually capable of acting more rationally. Certainly, a goodwilled sceptic might question whether the capacity to love necessarily renders a person rational in other areas, especially in areas of society where one has to deal with individuals one neither hates nor loves, areas where Reich's conduct was hardly exemplary or instructive. Why has there been none of this scepticism in the face of Reich's work? Both the people who reject or accept Reich's work have been content to go on their feelings. But feelings are no proof of the truth—although they may point to it.

Certainly, the total subordination to Reich's truth which often prevails among individuals who have undergone his therapy does not speak for an increase in rationality, neither does the doctrinaire and arrogant assumption that one has the truth which often accompanies it. Sometimes I fear that the softening, the increased capacity for pleasure and love brings with it a corresponding mental hardening which the individuals overcome by trying to tell themselves it is conviction. Certainly, there is something desperately wrong with the attitude that Reich's work says the last word on everything, which many individuals who are acquainted with it adopt.

Health finally means going it alone, without the answers. I think Reich knew that even as he hungered to understand everything. For that was breathing for him, to understand, to see, to touch. In fact he understood so much because he did not hang on to what he had understood, but began anew in a sense each day. It is a terrible irony but one that repeats and repeats, that his understanding is seized upon by some individuals to prevent their own.

I do not think that Reich's formulation of the distinction of the three layers of character is incorrect. Yet he abused his discovery of that truth when in its name he airily dismissed the conventions of the adult world, of the surface in which are taken, after all, the decisions and choices which count: life and death, marriage and begetting, distinguishing between friends and enemies, profession.

Often explicitly and almost always implicitly he dismissed the stuff of everyday life as nothing more than hypocritical lip service to what human beings could have been. To take such an attitude amounted to saying no one had lived before him, that it had up to then all been a dream, as Descartes dreaded.

But the truth is that wherever genuine living occurs, the hypocritical and real and rational struggle against each other and that to the extent that anything genuine and worthwhile is accomplished, it is accomplished because the surface has a genuine relation to what Reich called the core.

Of course, Reich knew this—but in some way also he denied it. As in much else of Reich's work, it is his insistence on the blanket validity of his conclusions that tends to distort them. In his readiness to dismiss the surface as sham, Reich fell into as deep and a more destructive error than those who leadenly maintain that nothing could be better than the way things are.

This attack on the surface, this refusal to deal with it on its own terms is typical of both communism and psychoanalysis, two movements with which Reich was associated. With Reich and probably most everybody who indulges it this insistence on going beneath the surface in order to deal with it and improve upon it had always a certain unacknowledged contempt and suspiciousness. For it tends to understand and in this sense of understanding, to dismiss a person before knowing him, on the authority of a theory. It is a contempt that in its refusal to know itself represents a driving force in twentieth century history. This contempt, this assurance of knowing without and before experience, has brought the great, the intelligent, the courageous out of their houses and mansions into the street to exile or death; it has hurled the statues from their bases; all only to create a self-enslaving idolatry of mind which is much more pervasive, more difficult to identify than what it has replaced.

The real problem with Reich's work is that some of what he says is true. That is why his work will not simply go away. The problem is what to do with this truth, how to live with it (rather than off it). As I remarked at the start, blind acceptance is, if anything, more grotesque than arbitrary rejection.

Reich himself did not know what to do with his truth. In all his work he is racing against something—sometimes it feels like nature herself who is as fleet and beautiful as a Greek goddess, but at other times it feels like some realization he wishes to avoid at all costs, lest it blacken his sight. I mean some realization about himself, some terror before doubt (the very doubt in which the contemporary world is born), some dread, not unlike Tolstoy's, that life itself will prove not to be enough. That is why he races with nature for the prize.

Also, there is in him, in his work, a fear of choking what he has to say, a fear of the emaciated silence of those who do not dare speak their mind—and that is a rational, even a noble fear (if there is such a thing). We all have it and some of us are drawn almost irresistibly to those who know they have it and speak out against it. It is the dread of the dimming of the eyes and dulling of the ears, of existing without knowing you see or hear, of life somehow being out of reach, of always being too late.

Reich's therapy gives one the chance to feel like a hero without taking any risks. It is imbued, more than any of Freud's work, with his defiant challenge at the beginning of *Interpretation of Dreams, si superos flectere nequeo, Acheronta movebo.* Not for nothing did Reich have Nietzsche always at his side, the way, I am tempted to add, Alexander carried the *Iliad* at his.

This yearning to be heroes without taking risks marks much of the youth of the upper ranks in the free West. It reflects all the ambiguity of dreading to give up privilege and yet fearing its responsibility. It explains the frantic paroxysms of educational institutions (whatever they are?) to be "relevant" and their growing fear of the facts of history. For above all heroism without risks is divorced from history and, therefore, for the most part from any relation to other men. It occurs in the mind; no, not in the mind, in the sensations. It has to do with what one feels, not with what one is. For it cannot conceive that one is not what one feels. That is it does not know facts.

Such a yearning for a heroism without risks drew individuals to Fascism and Nazism. One can still hear it here and there in the drawn, muttered breaths of Europe, "Better to live a day like a lion, than a thousand years as sheep." Because it did not know itself for what it was it led to self-immolation and murder. Reich knew all this and dreaded it. Like everybody alive now in the West he lived in the shadow of Nazism and Fascism and Communism. He said once in an astonishing remark, "I could have been a Führer like Hitler."[16] In varying degrees that is the story of us all. Yet he fed this desire for heroism without risks. Why?

Because he himself was a hero—of that I have no doubt, a tragic hero, like perhaps all heroes—but a hero who could not stand greatness and yet could not get along without it. That too in varying degrees is true of us all.

He did not want to be alone out there, he did not want to accept that you had to become a hero if you went out there, but he insisted on going out there. To resolve this ambiguity he wanted us all to accompany him. He did not want a crew, like Columbus, for his voyage, he wanted all mankind to follow him. He wanted us all to become Prometheans—and forgot, and it is a terrible thing to forget although it is the kind of thing that goes forgotten all the time in the twentieth century, that Prometheus was an old god and that even that was barely enough to make for his survival.

But there is more to it than that. In some sense Reich could not live with the realization that heroism like freedom must occur of its own, must run the risk of error, that there are no formulas for it, because it occurs in specific circumstances which do not repeat. He could not accept that heroism was something you did at your own risk and for which there are no recipes and no tangible rewards.

In some sense he wanted to teach others to be like himself, because he feared to be himself. Also he could not live without hoping, which meant for him feeling the life in others, that is at its rudest, poking them to see if they would squirm.

But towards the end of his life Reich grew close to

terrified of the confidence and great expectations of his youth and manhood—somehow they had let him down. He reviled men for their earlier expectations of him, for having believed what he said, for having believed in him. But it was largely in fear of self. Perhaps in some simple sense life grew monstrous in him, and to him, especially in the face of death, because he loved it so much and so closely.

Had he lived in antiquity he would have had a cult as a hero upon his death and that would have ended it, but in our time there are no heroes except in words and in the mind and so I write this essay.

Energy

If it is correct, the discovery of orgone energy completes Reich's work on orgasm and Freud's crucial work on sexuality. At present the only significant, indubitable fact about Reich's work on energy is that in forty years nobody has attempted an objective evaluation, and repeated Reich's experiments. This neglect, this readiness to dismiss what might be crucial experimental work without verifying it tells something serious about our attitude towards knowledge and our actual relation to the intellectual traditions, the traditions of the Reformation and the Enlightenment, we live off. It also tells something about the relation of much of our research to wonder—to the capacity to ask basic questions. Since when has it been the style to deal with major work, with perhaps major defects, by dismissing it or embracing it out of hand!

Reich's disciples, it is true, have repeated some of his experiments, but they are so committed beforehand to accepting rigidly every last thing Reich said and so incapable of facing the possibility that Reich may have been wrong about some things that they do little more than mechanically repeat Reich's conclusions. Even if Reich were right about everything, which is highly unlikely, wholesale acceptance of his work, essentially because one dreads to question it, hardly amounts to an effective way of finding out whether Reich actually discovered something. The most effective criticism and acceptance of any work is further work which confirms it by modifying it.

With Reich there has been very little work of this sort. There have been repetitions and denials, most of them arbitrary, but with the exception of some important work on vision by Elsworth Baker which, however, remains fully within the context of Reich's assumptions and, therefore, his limitations, there has been little advance.[17]

Great work is always difficult to accept or reject. Maybe Reich's work on energy is too simple and obvious. Certainly, if Reich turns out to have been right about orgone energy, it will be mighty embarrassing to explain to oneself how it happened that something so obvious could have been ignored for centuries. Of course it will be said that fundamental discoveries (when they are comprehensible) have always been of obvious things. But with orgone energy it is all much harder, because much more obvious. For instance I do not think one can know one is alive without in some sense perceiving (or at least conceiving) energy. Again, I suddenly find myself starting at the ghost of Descartes who wondered whether he lived or dreamt.

In an oblique sense much Western philosophy makes reference to what Reich called orgone energy. Most basically the overwhelming perception of the coherence of world and nature, the sense that space is full and life meaningful amounts to something close to the perception of orgone energy, except that it is in some sense always metaphorical. The whole Christian effort to keep in some contact with God, and even more so the classical sense that there is a reality and nature without whose experience it is impossible to live, as opposed to merely exist, all point to something very close to "orgone energy" or the way individuals experience "orgone energy."

Reich himself considered the Christian striving for contact with God, as well as the metaphysical passion of philosophy, as mystical and evasive and finally more damaging than the mechanistic, scientific approach which has been its antithesis. He thought, I think, that the mechanistic and exclusively empirical approach, for all its mindlessness and possible consequent brutality, by ridding itself of all presuppositions, cleared the field for fundamental discoveries for those whose eyes and minds were clear enough to make them. The point was that with the scientific methodology men would get whatever knowledge they deserved. In contrast the metaphysical mode, because it assumed it knew something before it learned and experienced it, could never really discover that what it knew happened to be actually true.[18]

I think the neglect of Reich's work on cancer represents, in part, a fear of coherence, of actually understanding the disease in meaningful terms. It also, however, reflects the at the same time more superficial and practical and profounder problem of all Reich's work that it is probably impossible to deal with any aspect of Reich's work without facing and understanding all his previous work. And this means facing an uncomfortable connection between self-knowledge and what one is and what one discovers and understands. It also means deep involvement with Reich's character and the passion of his life and in some sense his own lack of self-knowledge, for as always the man Reich is with difficulty distinguishable and separable from his work.

Not only does Reich's work on cancer demand that one know something of oneself but also that one cope with Reich and with his inability to cope with himself. If fundamental scientific knowledge could be pursued without such involvement with self and world the reluctance of few if any researchers to deal with Reich's work on cancer would be comprehensible. It cannot. The confident assumption of many of our scientists that they can face and answer fundamental questions without risking their lives amounts to desiring the fruits of knowledge without facing its consequences. There is no way to achieve fundamental knowledge innocently—without first having come apart and gone through the refining fire. In fact I suspect that scientists who are unaware that the fundamental knowledge they pursue entails risking their lives inadvertently risk the lives of their worlds.

I mean that the extremity of our political situation which threatens us daily with annihilation bears some inverted relation to the illusion of many of our men of knowledge that they can pursue fundamental knowledge without facing themselves and without risking their lives and property. If Reich's life and work (in some sense they are inseparable) teaches anything, it teaches that fundamental knowledge cannot be pursued without facing oneself, that is, without risking one's life.

Politics

It would probably tell a great deal about Reich if one could come to an understanding of his political activity independent of his own understanding of it. In fact without such an understanding it is impossible to evaluate his remarkable work on irrationality in politics. For this work is, as his work almost always is, in part an unacknowledged defense of his life and his way of doing things. Politics was perhaps the area in which Reich made his biggest errors and faced them in part when he was forced to. He would not have survived if he had not.

The wonder is that Reich ever imagined his understanding as a physician could quickly change a political situation. In part it was Reich's impatience that rendered him so susceptible to the illusion that his general understanding of the causes of submissiveness could help individuals achieve independence almost immediately. In its turn this impatience represented Reich's way of living with the political crisis which surrounded him and which, like all crises, demanded action. It is difficult to tell to what extent this sense of urgency, this sense of having to change everything immediately, was a genuine response rather than merely a manifestation within his character of the general political crisis.

But there is more to it than this. In some real sense Reich could not distinguish rational obedience from submissiveness. For him all obedience more or less amounted to submissiveness. As a result, also like many of his generation, he was astonishingly casual about the terrible costs of revolt and even defiance. By coming close to confusing all obedience with submissiveness, Reich in effect obscured the necessity for choosing between defiance and obedience in any particular situation.

By acting and thinking as if there was no choice, Reich fostered the illusion that individuals were not responsible for their actions almost as much as if he had insisted on unconditional obedience. Somehow I think it is this tendency to take all obedience for submissiveness which allowed Reich to pasture in the illusion of relatively easy solutions. It was almost as if he imagined everything would be alright if only individuals did not think. But they do and this is what distinguishes them from animals. Saying individuals could be free if they did not think, amounts to saying individuals could be free if they did not live like free men. In fact in an important sense Reich would not distinguish between human beings and animals. For instance, he did not wonder that human beings spoke.

Although after his expulsion from the Communist party and his break with Communism and Marxism, Reich rewrote his political works, which he had in part conceived in Marxist and Communist terms, his rewriting amounts really to expurgation. For specific Communist or Marxist slogans he substituted vaguer phrases about progress. The animus, the set of mind, especially the will to defiance, is still the same, only not so knowing of itself, not so undisguised. Reich did not really face the intellectual consequences of his break.

There is no sign, for instance, that after he dropped his Marxist presuppositions, Reich turned to an independent study of history or of the political thinkers such as Adam Smith or David Ricardo who preceded Marx. After his break with Communism, Marx remained Reich's only author in history and statecraft, not because he believed him, but because he would know no other. I suspect Reich needed Marx, needed his reductionism. He held on to him, even after he had taken his distance from him, by not reading other authors who might teach him Marx's limitations (I am thinking of Aristotle's crucial refutation of the arguments for the abolition of property and the family in the second book of the *Politics.)*

Just as for many of his followers Reich is the only author, so Reich himself seems to have needed to devote himself to one author at the expense of others. His hunger for conviction, for elemental assurance was such that he feared living doubt, the doubt which arises when one understands that men of stature and goodwill think differently. For Reich difference of opinion implied frivolity and neurotic distortion.

Dread of the thought of others which moves of its own sweet will probably rendered Reich so reluctant to face up to actual *bona fide* differences of judgement and opinion. It was as if he feared his own convictions would vanish in the countering presence of the words of others. This dread of the thought of others lent his own thought a kind of stubborn rusticity—he wrote often as if no one had written or thought before him—which is pretty close to the opposite counterpart of the sophistry he hated.

Of the scars of his Communist experience, the ugliest was the persuasion he bore to the end of his life that all politics was irrational. The truth was that the two movements he had studied, Communism and Nazism, one of which he had been involved in, were irrational; but it did not follow from this that all politics was irrational. Reich's readiness to assert that *all* political movements are irrational because he had suffered severely in some, betrays some of his arrogance, and some of his resignation and some of his cynicism. His extravagant hopes, his unwillingness to concede that there was any necessary distinction between what one could imagine and what one could actually do, have some relation to this resignation; they are its other side. In some sense Reich scorned the possible, the necessarily little steps which taken together lead somewhere.

In short, although he no longer professed the change of society by revolutionary means, he still kept himself outside and above the constitution. He would not be a citizen. At the heart of this self-exclusion, which amounted to an unwillingness to accept his political equality with other men, quite analogous to his reluctance to deal with his professional peers, there is the fear I have already mentioned of learning anything from anybody else.

One can sense something of the arrogance of Reich's

assertions of quietism and resignation when one realizes that Reich began to indulge in them more or less upon his arrival in the United States in 1939, the first country he was to live in for any length of time which had a republican constitution which had survived more than a generation, that is the first country he had ever lived in in which parents could look their children in the eyes, and children their parents, without laying the world about them to waste.

Reich's stance of resigned and somewhat cynical aloofness and isolation, in Reich's instance, represents a reaction to the frightful collapse of Europe. Among his American adherents this resignation betrays something more sinister than innocence or ignorance of historical context. It tells of an inability to witness their country's life because of ideological presuppositions.

His adherence to Communism also probably reinforced Reich's inability to tolerate criticism and opposition, his insistence that all must agree with him, his fear of the freespokenness of others. It made his later conservatism, for instance, his exaggerated faith (I use the word advisedly) in General Eisenhower, always have something of the vehemence, rigidity and lability of conversion.

Because he did not distinguish his political from his professional work, Reich never imagined politics had anything more to do with him than the pathology of anyone of his private patients. That is, he did not understand the difference between citizenship and the exercise of a profession, between political freedom and healing. More significantly, he could not conceive—or would not admit—the capacity of a free society to correct itself, to undermine and check the irrational tendencies of its individual members. As a result he could not conceive of himself in *a* world in distinction to *the* world, for professionals live in the world but citizens in a country. Most concretely, and in significant contrast to Socrates, this meant he would not admit of not being judge in his own case. In some important sense he would not trust anybody outside of himself—which can only mean that in the end he did not trust himself.

It is difficult also to tell to what degree Reich's remarkable grasp of the irrational element in Fascism and Nazism—written and published, it should not be forgotten, in the middle of events—depended on his Marxism and Communism, difficult to tell to what extent his clear grasp of the reactionary destructive character of Nazism depended on his blindness to the corresponding irrationality of Communism. For instance, his clear grasp of how rigid authoritarian, ascetically-minded families tended to destroy young people's capacity for independence and self-confidence relied heavily on the Marxist and Communist conception of the family as nothing more than a reflection of the oppressive state in miniature. Although Reich elaborated the conception of a natural family in contrast to the compulsive family, which stayed together only because husband and wife feared to go it alone, Reich never granted the actual family much rationality. He would not face the fact that the effective and constructive individuals in the world had grown to be what they were in part because they had been blessed enough to be born in families in which love was palpable. Finally, I think he envied such individuals. They were the real "bourgeoisie". In a psychological sense that is always what the bourgeoisie is in Communist propaganda, individuals who have reason to love their parents and know it.

When Reich spoke of the natural family he spoke of it as something that might come to be in the future, not as something you could occasionally see around you. As in much of his writing, this emphasis on the future tended to encourage his readers in the rejection of the present and reenforce their inability to cope with it.

In fact when he looked out upon the present, Reich came perilously close to arguing that the contemporary family should be abolished to prevent the formation of the Oedipus complex. But his priggish remark that he was as remarkable as he was because he had had a good mama indicates his harsh criticism of the family was not entirely aboveboard. How could anybody's be?[20] In some sense Reich was arguing nobody else except him had had parents.

Of course in time—and, it should be emphasized, long before it made itself plain in the Stalin-Ribbentrop Pact—Reich realized the substantial inverted agreement between Nazism and Communism. He did not, however, as I have pointed out, see how deeply such a realization challenged his previous thought. It was as if Reich chose to retire from the world in the face of his realization of the irrationality of the two extremes of Fascism and Communism rather than experience the rationality of the mean, by which I mean the rationality of free societies. In fact, Reich's increased concentration on biology and physics dates more or less from the middle thirties, the time when the irrationality of both Nazism and Communism bore in upon him. From that time on Reich thought somehow nature would allow him to bypass man. In contrast, facing the mean would have meant facing history, that is, what men had done, without theoretical or ideological preconceptions, something Reich yearned to do but dared not.

In some real sense Reich was arguing that, since Europe was destroyed, we had to live in the state of nature. But he did not realize this, for he did not realize that anybody had spoken of these problems before him. In terms of classical political thought, with which Reich seems to have been unacquainted, Reich wanted a return to the benign state of nature of Locke rather than the grim one of Hobbes.

One has to ask oneself why Reich should have, more or less unawares, found in catastrophe the grounds for greater optimism and greater demands of life. The vehemence of his hope marks the intensity of the despair he was fighting off. In this readiness to make disaster the ground of great expectations he is typical of his time. For the chiliastic expectation of a new world to spring from the ashes of the old which was made to justify the Second World War keeps us from the sobering experience of its tragedy. Certainly, there is something odd, even desperate, in making disaster the ground of great expectations? Because they are grounded in previous failure rather than success, such expectations can lead to much worse than what came before them.

A deeper knowledge of what had happened in the past might have prompted Reich to wonder whether his struggle in the face of disaster to find freedom in nature and even to aspire to a greater freedom than had preceded disaster and to define it in an unjuridical sense that bordered on being antijuridical did not amount to an evasion of the hard fact that it is hard, if not impossible, as Rousseau thought, for peoples to reacquire freedom once they have lost it.

Although Reich argued that sexual freedom, as distinguished from sexual license, would increase an individual's capacity for rationality, his teaching fears reason, the independent movement of dialogue, and tries to substitue sensation for it and for language. He did not realize that a world which tended to substitute sensation for reason ran the risk of turning into a world in which men were slaves to their sensations. It could also easily turn into a world in which one individual did not talk to another, that is, a world in which individuals could not learn from one another. And a world in which individuals cannot learn from each other is also a world in which they cannot teach themselves. In an important sense it is a world in which every man thinks he is the only one. A crowd—for no such world could make up a polity—in which everyone thinks he is the only one—that is pretty close to the essence of tyranny.

Free societies (polities), in contrast, disappoint one of one's vain illusions. They teach one that there is sometimes a difference between one's sensations and the facts. They free you from your narcissism and teach you that living one's own life means acknowledging the lives of others. (I am almost reducing citizenship to manners or to the grace which quickens manners.)

In some important sense Reich kept denying all this, he kept denying that anybody else but himself could live. He wanted freedom, but he wanted it without other people to disappoint him, to question him, to surprise him with what occurred to them. And that amounts to not wanting it at all. In some way he wished to overpower life with his thought, for he feared its disappointments, even as he taught its unexpectedness.

Partly because Reich conceived of freedom in unjuridical terms (at least until the very end of his life, when he grew interested in natural law), he tended to equate it with limitlessness. But the insistence on limitless freedom which goes with the tendency to conceive of freedom in terms of the capacity for pleasure and love of life can be easily turned into, perverted is perhaps the word, a yearning for tyranny, for a tyranny no less tyrannical because many think they are free in it.

In fact, significantly, Reich could not conceive of a situation in which men thought they were free but were actually slaves. For him what was crucial was that men feel free. But it is precisely in totalitarian societies that many men *feel* free, and in free societies that many, especially among the young and the university and intellectual "elites," feel enslaved.[21] For real freedom does not aim to please. In contrast to tyranny it does not flatter; it disappoints. It teaches over and over again that there is a difference between what one wishes for and what one thinks one is and what one actually is—and that life lives in the difference. That is it teaches that one must drop one's preconceptions of oneself, one's conceit and narcissism, if one is to discover what one has become. Most importantly, it brings it home to one almost daily that if one is to move at all one must move of one's own.

In fact I would say that one of the marks of real freedom is its capacity to make many individuals who are not up to its responsibilities and its pleasures—and that means in varying degrees almost everybody—feel in some sense enslaved. That is why there is so much superficial, but for all that not less corrosive, bitterness and desecration in the happiest countries, why some of the free so fervently profess their slavery and envy actual slaves their freedom.

Instead, Reich tended to equate freedom with what one thinks and feels—and this too although distinct from, is perilously close to, totalitarianism. For the point about political and juridical freedom is that it frees one somewhat from the burden of one's fantasies and involuntary thoughts and tells one that one's actions (including one's spoken words) are what counts. And there is a lot in that, for if one's acts are appropriate and effective, one's thoughts will to some extent take care of themselves.

In contrast, the insistence on limitless freedom and the equation of freedom with pleasure, when it becomes an ideology, must lead to tyranny because it denies the distinction between one individual and another and with it the sense of individual responsibility for one's life and thus renders all susceptible to idolatry (the so-called "cult of personality"). I mean Reich dreaded the judgement of his peers.

In a passage attempting to come to terms with the spread and persistence of Soviet despotism, which is the unfinished business of all our lives, Nadezhda Mandelstam provides a powerful criticism of Reich's conception of freedom. I would like to say it is only a criticism of the distortions which Reich's conception of freedom is heir to—but somehow these distortions appear to me to inhere in the conception itself:

> People who were silent or closed their eyes to what was happening also try to make excuses for the past. They generally accuse me of subjectivism, saying that I see only one side of the picture and ignore all the other things: the building up of industry, Meyerhold's stage productions, the Cheliuskin expedition and so forth. None of this, to my mind, absolves us from our duty to make sense of what happened. *We have lived through a severe crisis of nineteenth-century humanism during which all its ethical values collapsed because they were*

> *founded only on man's needs and desires, his longing for personal happiness.* The twentieth century has also shown us that evil has an enormous urge to self-destruction. It inevitably ends in total folly and suicide. Unfortunately, as we now understand, in destroying itself, evil may destroy all life on earth as well. However much we shout about these elementary truths, they will only be heeded by people who themselves want no more of evil. None of this, after all, is new: everything is always repeated, though on an ever greater scale. Luckily, I shall not see what the future holds in store.
> (Underlining mine.)[22]

Within the limits and reservations of these criticisms it is Reich's imperishable merit to have grasped the connection between servility (including the inability to think independently) and the incapacity to experience and feel love. For the first time he understood the role of enforced asceticism, especially in adolescence, in making destructive and insecure individuals.

At the heart of this enterprise is a desire, in part unacknowledged, to lay bare the roots of the murder and destruction in the twentieth century. Like (in one way or another) almost everybody, Reich wanted to free himself from the burden of the time of his life—but strangely he tried to do this not through history, but almost exclusively through a study of the self. Because of this exclusivity and the inability to conceive of politics with a rational core his work on politics is, to a limited but important extent, a symptom of the crisis it seeks to understand.

Especially towards the end of his life, Reich grew alarmed at the damage which comes of compulsive promiscuity, especially of the arrogance and contempt it tends to stimulate—but in general his work is not conscious enough of the limitations and the dangers of its own understanding. It is not noted for the modesty of its claims—and one does not do it honor by accepting these claims at face value.

During the last twenty years in the United States many young people have tried to live in accordance with ideas concerning pleasure and love close to Reich's. It is difficult to tell how programmatic this effort to have a more positive and straightforward attitude toward pleasure was. My impression is that Reich's work had little directly to do with it. But his ideas, disguised and distorted, reached the young through the pansexualism of Paul Goodman and Norman Mailer.

Much confusion has come with this effort to change inherited ways. I have often had the sense of people, both parents and children, trying to talk themselves out of the way they really feel. That is why there is a widespread, gnawing sense of unease and many blank looks. Also, this effort has been connected, in my judgement necessarily, with a great deal of rigid and programmatic opinionatedness about politics, and something approaching a hatred for facts and a will to substitute sensation for them—a tendency which now is sweeping high schools.

All this recent experience modifies Reich's early view that sexual freedom was somehow a prerequisite of political freedom. It suggests rather that questions of sexual freedom arise as a consequence of political freedom, especially in the United States, where great victories have imposed world-wide responsibilities of leadership which cannot be lived up to without self-knowledge. What we have lived through also suggests that any attempt to adopt a more flexible attitude toward sexuality and, finally, a more honest and discriminating attitude toward love, will strain a free country's capacity for freedom to the utmost before reenforcing it. And we do not know yet whether it does in fact reenforce it.

WORK AND LIFE: CONCLUSIONS

Work And Life: Conclusions

It was as if in his work Reich would substitute nature for man, because he had such contempt for him (or, as he would have put it, for what he had made of himself), and feared him so much. But in man there was also himself and in fleeing him Reich also fled himself, his tragedy, his rootlessness, his sense that he belonged neither to heaven or earth. In this too he was a child of Europe, of twentieth-century Europe turned fatally against herself, a child driven over half the earth from one country to another where he would find nothing familiar or intimate to see or hear. As a result, in all the courage of discovery of these years, there is always an unmistakeable sense of flight, evasion, and terror, and it is not entirely terror before the magnificence of heaven and earth which opened up to his eyes. When he is most critical of man, most fierce against him, in these years, there is always something of prayer about it, as if he were hoping he would find someone with a voice mighty enough to call him to himself.

There is flight too in Reich's attitude in therapy. He was interested in the protoplasm in a person, in what he was like when he did not talk, in the way he breathed, and in the way he touched, he was interested in what made him a part of nature, not so much in what made him able to distinguish himself from the rest of nature, not in what allowed him to answer to a name. In fact he is weakest in his theory of consciousness. This is crucial in understanding his work, and in perceiving its limitations (something he was altogether incapable of doing, as perhaps most geniuses are).[23]

For Reich, self-awareness or consciousness occurred only because man feared his sensations. Consciousness was a function of his fear of life and in some sense, therefore, painful, and forced upon himself unwittingly, not unlike something slowly tightening about him. For Reich consciousness meant man's fear of himself. It would not have occurred if he had not walled off from life and stiffened to it. In short Reich did not have a theory of consciousness he could distinguish from armour. His theory of consciousness, which in the end conceives of consciousness as a defect, strikes one of the harshest false notes in his work, whose limits otherwise must be sought mostly in what he did not understand and did not know he did not understand.

What Reich discovered was the nature of other men, of men other than himself. That is why his discoveries were compatible with flight from other men and society. In this he contrasts with Socrates, who knew whatever he knew of the self because he faced himself. It is because of this contrast, because Reich discovered much about the self without knowing himself, that he could not—in contrast again to Socrates—recognize the authority of the court before which he was accused. In a sense this desire of knowledge of nature without self-knowledge is inherent in what we call science. As a result science reflects both what we are and what we have turned ourselves into without knowing it.

Reich at least modified that tradition when he approached nature through knowledge of the self, though not through knowledge of himself. For all that, if one desires to understand why Socrates (who knew the force of knowledge meant the experience of ignorance), could say there was one thing he knew about, that was desire, one can best learn it from Reich.

Reich's unwillingness to experience individual life has some relation to the weakness of his theory of consciousness. In his view all individuals belonged to one irrational type or another. When faced with critics objecting to this reductionism (in a rare instance when he did actually answer his critics, that is talk to someone who was not his patient), Reich replied with some impatience that everybody fell into one irrational typology or the other, even though they were in some sense unique.

This resort to typology would not be so disturbing if Reich had remained simply a doctor. For against a background of a firm experience of health as the normal condition, diseases can be distinguished with some confidence. But when fairly on (probably sometime between the composition of the first edition of *Function of the Orgasm,* 1927, and *Character Analysis,* 1933) Reich began to believe almost everyone was more or less deeply disturbed, he ceased to be a physician in any meaningful sense. No longer able to refer to health as in some sense a general experience, he came perilously close to asserting he was the only one who had any experience of it. In such a context the application of typology to almost everybody he met, to all patients at any rate (and whom did he meet except patients?) meant he put himself in a position where he more or less continually risked entrapment in his theories.[24] There could be little that would surprise him once he sheltered behind the assumption of universal disease. Who was to cure *him?* I do not think he ever faced these and other consequences of abandoning the usual distinctions between health and disease.

With Reich it is difficult to tell where the hate stops and the love starts, whether his hatred of the neurotic distortions in man does not come perilously close to a hatred of life, the life of men at any rate. Certainly, the struggle between life and death within Reich was very deep, and he would have done well to acknowledge it in himself at the same time he pointed it out so fiercely in others. His lack of willingness to acknowledge in himself what he pointed out in others is also related to his reluctance to see anything rational in consciousness. I am saying that this man who could help men find nature in themselves and, therefore, know it also outside themselves, in some sense feared self-knowledge and reason. His truth was also a way of not knowing something about himself and his insistence on never talking to anybody on their own terms or even in the common terms of discourse (for he came close to inventing his own language) represented also a fear of self-knowledge, of experiencing the edges of himself. Above all he feared life might disappoint his truth, as it disappoints all truth in order to keep "Truth" from enslaving it.

In some intuitive sense Reich's most prominent disciple, Elsworth Baker, realizes that the weakest aspect of Reich's work has to do with consciousness, for he has done important work on the armouring of the eyes, the kind of blocking in sight, especially in the perception of depth, which prevents an individual from seeing what is going on before him and about him in the world, and making accurate judgements about it.[25] Translated into less general terms, this amounts to a covert acknowledgement that the largest problems of this therapy have to do with the patient's relation to the world of men, just as it was Reich's own most crucial problem. In fact Reich's inability to see the world of men and his place in it drove him to view most of society and history as irrational.

In the context of his time, especially of his youth (1914) Reich's readiness to reduce thought to something approaching sensation makes some sense. At least it is comprehensible. For Reich was growing up from a world which had broken upon its too-easily-assumed confidence in its rationality. By emphasizing the relation of thought to what a person felt, saw and was, Reich tried to learn and to teach the distinction between thought and rationalization, that is the abuse of reason to justify irrationality. But now when few people can think, to reduce thought to no more than sensation amounts to stressing the irrational at a time when people are all too ready to take it for granted. In fact without some recognition of rationality it is impossible to experience emotion, such as love, as distinguished from sensation, such as desire. Reich knew what he was talking about when he warned the truths of one generation risked becoming the lies of the next.

Reich spoke readily of a ruined humanity and felt himself compelled, as I have pointed out in discussing his political work, even to attack the past in order to defend his truth. In fact in some real sense it was the past that threatened him most. Even though it could no longer speak—although it could be heard by those who would listen—Reich feared it and I think rightly. For the past is what we would learn of the future if we could see it. It is the great disabuser of those who take their love of life for immortality, their innocence for courage, their good intentions for prudence, who wish to think that originality means thinking something nobody else has thought before.

Reich's fear of history, his inability to understand the marvel of speech and language (for him it was largely a means of evasion) and his reluctance to experience the rationality of the way people actually lived (to the extent that they do live) are all interconnected, and point to the limits and defects of his understanding.

This amounts to saying Reich remained always a scientist, interested in the general, and the specific only to the extent that it exemplified the general, somehow not able to cope with the unique which is somehow what language, history and society reflect, the fact that life is everywhere different and unexpected and unpredictable and only finally to be lived in the first and second person and not in the third, which is the person of scientific work.

I doubt too that any deep experience of rationality and consciousness is possible without dialogue, that is without some sense of language and of its reciprocity, that is, of speaking as well as listening, and I doubt that dialogue is possible without an implicit experience of society and, thereby, of history. Instead Reich was interested in telling people the truth and discovering its immutable laws. That is, he wanted to bring natural science into areas of judgement and courage where a man, whoever he was, had finally to come to his own decision by his own lights.

In some sense Reich was astonished that anybody else lived. He was at the same time overwhelmed by the realization that the people he saw were alive and by a harsh sense of their inability to live, of their disabilities. With this there came a terrific impulse to judge, a lordly impulse. Underneath all his love of freedom there was an even more powerful yearning for authority. He protested his love of freedom, because he feared his devotion to authority and probably suspected his capacity to distinguish between authority and authoritarianism. I think this yearning had to do with the authority he had experienced in his youth in Austria-Hungary of before the First World War.

But this yearning for authority was not something he could admit to himself, for the life of his early adulthood was to a large extent founded on the rejection of the world of his youth which had been destroyed in the War.

At most one can catch his yearning for authority in his hatred of the abuse of freedom. He hated license, that is the abuse of most noble freedoms for the worst ends, for instance the abuse of free speech as a justification of pornography. In this he was noble. He craved for a world with real authority and real leadership, the leadership and authority that had proved itself hollow in the First World War and had been murderously parodied by Fascism, Communism, and Nazism in its aftermath. It is hard to say how conscious of this he was.

In a sense the whole history of his life can be summed up in the very slowly and hesitantly formulated sense that finally the Austro-Hungarian Empire and the other old regimes had a deeper sense of fairplay and honesty, perhaps because they knew their limitations, and did not promise everything, than the revolutionary regimes fashioned in war, which strove to succeed them by improving upon them. He never said as much, and perhaps would have disagreed with any such statement even at the end, but the recognition of the integrity of the world before the First World War is the final lesson of his work. In the end his work teaches, if only inadvertently, the necessity of leadership, that is of upper classes who are capable of understanding the justification of their privileges lies in the burden of their responsibilities.

Reich did not recognize his origins. This too has to do with his readiness to dismiss history, consciousness and language. In all his writings there is hardly an autobiographical remark, any indication that he, like other men, had had a father or mother. I suddenly think of the magnificent appearance of the father of Ulysses in the vegetable patch at the end of the *Odyssey*. But Reich was a wanderer who never came home.

The tone in Reich's work is always impersonal, distant, scientific—I would say cold, but it is not. It is all somehow based on the assumption that the author is unquestionably and inexplicably different.[26] This is all the more remarkable and at the same time all the more comprehensible when one considers that Reich's work touches on every conceivable human intimacy. He wanted it all out, but that included nothing about himself.

Like Oedipus, Reich acted as if he came from nowhere. Hardly ever does he talk of his homeland. He lived for twenty years in America, but in all his writings there is hardly a remark that indicates he experienced the difference between Europe and America, that he knew the feel of an American street, that he could sense the matter-of-fact unassuming American warmth and innocence which can at times be a most effective masque for cunning.

His third wife writes of his not liking to attend chamber music concerts in New York, because it bothered him to come upon the old crowd of Austrian and German refugees, the friends and acquaintances of his youth.[27] It is a petty detail but revealing, for it again seems to testify to his unwillingness to face his origins, to his readiness to isolate himself, to act as if he came from nowhere—and also to an almost primordial shyness.

One would never guess from Reich's works that at the age of nineteen he had been an officer in the army of the Hapsburg Empire on the Italian front and, more astonishing still, that he had enjoyed command.[28] That was a world he wished to forget, that he had to forget. In some sense that was true of everybody who had lived through those times. To draw one's breath in pain at the world of one's grandparents and parents—that is the cost of surviving catastrophe. But Reich had more than the usual reasons for blindness to his youth. In an important sense he was a man who had to be reborn, who dared no longer know the name of his parents or the country he was born in.

Reich had good reason not to want to have anything to do with *his* past—which he perhaps did not distinguish from *the* past—better reason than the simple historical catastrophe of the First World War which broke the European world in half.

When he was about fourteen he told his father of the affair his mother was having with his tutor. She committed suicide. Sometime later Reich's father succumbed to tuberculosis which developed from a pneumonia he had contracted by standing in a pond for hours in cold weather "ostensibly," as Reich's third wife puts it, fishing.[29]

The facts are brutal. But they do not speak for themselves—entirely. I do not know how to be discreet in their face. But I am sure prudence and discretion in this instance and in these circumstances do not mean silence. I have heard in unverifiable manner (third or fourth hand) that Reich's father mercilessly threatened Reich even physically before he told on his mother and his teacher.

I am astonished that Reich, who was relentless in his demands for honesty in his patients and on others, who hunted after the slightest hesitation, who probably could not distinguish between discretion and irrational secrecy, who wanted it all out, every dirty little secret, every concealed murderous feeling—so that his patients could breathe freely and sweetly without clenching their fists—never faced up to these facts in public. He wrote always as if the only burdens he shouldered were the burdens of other people. This refusal to acknowledge his own difficulties when he insisted on pointing out those of others is all the more remarkable when one remembers he was, as he once called himself, "a seasoned man of public affairs." Reich, however, took "public" to mean laying bare the privacy of others. There were to be no secrets. But public only means something when it is contrasted with private. For Reich instead "public" came perilously close to meaning the absence of privacy. In his own respect, he acted as if he had no private life. This meant not that he was frank and open about his own private life but that he fled from it into his kind of public life.

Instead of looking at his own life in public as he looked at the lives of others, Reich acted as if he had been born parentless and nameless, as if he came from nowhere. It is, for instance, difficult to imagine any place on earth he could bring himself to call his own, any place he dared call home. He acted as if it was unthinkable to question him, as if he had been born of nature. But to some extent his ferocity towards others, his insistence that they tell all, represented terror before his own privacy. As he put it somewhat arrogantly, he hated small talk.[30]

These facts which Reich never faced up to in public tell a lot. With such a past behind him a man would be driven to heroic deeds in order simply to survive. They tell of Reich's strange distance and formality which approached aloofness. They tell of his drive, at times savage and vengeful, to break into every private recess, to expose everything, to tell it all, to doubt the reality of everything that met his eyes. They tell also of his suspicion of the relation between parents and children and of the depth of the break his therapy tends to make between parents and children, husbands and wives. They tell also of Reich's demand that everything come apart before it could know itself in innocence to be sole or whole.

Circumstances had forced such disintegration on him and he would force it upon others. But had he come to terms with it in himself? His silence about his life speaks against that. He wanted all to become orphans in order that they might become by free choice the sons and daughters of their parents, that is distinguish themselves from them in order to know their relation to them. But somehow those who understand Reich at all come perilously close to becoming his sons and daughters (which helps to explain why Reichian organizations often feel like conspiratorial parties or like families or cults rather than scientific organizations, and why they cannot tolerate opposition or criticism).

Reich's inability to come to some sort of straightforward relation to these facts in a public manner tells also of the deep ambiguity at the heart of his work, of its daring and readiness to face all and yet of its evasiveness, of its inability to give its due to everyday wisdom and commonsense which grows upon one when one deals with one circumstance after the other. It tells also of the strange alternation within him of the highest aspirations for man and outrageous contempt for him. Each grew in a different way from his outrage at the present, and attempted to resolve or at least palliate its inner contradiction, for Reich hated in the present both what was worthy of hate and what should have moved him to awe, the mute facts of life moving of its own sweet will, which grew more undeniable the more one denied them.

Reich's reluctance to deal with himself and publicly face the particular facts of his life helps also to explain the strange mixture of flight and freedom in his work, especially its tendency to lead individuals away from the world of men at the same time that it brings them to nature and themselves. It helps also to explain his strange insistence on intimacy in the third person—for the second and the first would have compelled him to acknowledge the prosaic and terrible facts of his life and live in their presence. Instead he chose to study the facts which repeat, but always in part because he feared the facts that do not, the ones that make one life indelibly different from another and make the sweetest of pleasures, social intercourse, a telling reminder of the distinction between one life and another.

Reich's unacknowledged fear of experiencing his own measure lies close to the center of the crisis of the end of his life, a crisis he pointed to only in fleeting manner and perhaps did not know to be his own as well as mankind's. I sense it in his repeated remark that one dies alone, but it finds its most telling expression in *The Murder of Christ,* one of his last works, and the first one in which he comes close to experiencing himself as an author, rather than a natural scientist or a physician.[31]

In this work, meant in some way as an acknowledgement of the life-long company he kept with *Also Sprach Zarathustra,* there is an unmistakeable tone, which is difficult to name with one word. It is the tone which prevades the whole end of Reich's life. I would call it forlorn, but that too, like pessimism, is much too hopeful a word, for somehow it suggests the expectation of relief. Reich's mood at this time is much more fundamental, fundamental enough to paralyze easy expectations. What I perhaps mean is dread, foreboding, a dread that reached his innards. Reich at this time is like a person who dreads to hope, because he knows the consequences of hope.

This quality came, I think, from a sense that there was something that would not give, at which his words pounded but without answer—for the answer would have to come from himself to himself if it were to come at all. Instead he had always given the answers to everybody else. But now the answers had to come to himself from himself, because there was nobody else he would talk to. But because he could not talk to anybody else, he could not bring himself to talk to himself. Unable to address himself, he tried to address all mankind for perhaps the first time (with the possible exception of *Listen, Little Man!*) in something approaching the first person.[32] In this way, he sought to address himself, without realizing it, and thereby without listening to himself. Artists can do this, but Reich was not an artist. Somehow he was at a loss for words, for words that meant something to him, for words that could surprise him.

As a result he still addressed patients, not individuals. No matter whom he talked to, he saw patients; and once they became patients they confirmed his findings. Finally it turned out he spoke to still his own rising realization, to cry out against what he had to tell himself, because he could listen to no other. Because of this unstated conflict between what he told others and what he had to tell himself but could not, I read *Murder of Christ* with a harrowing sense that there is no way out for anybody who, like Reich, wanted to show the way out to others (in the end to everybody), but cannot somehow show it to himself. I think the passion of Christ drew Reich because he felt things closing in on him. There is a disturbing, bloody, terrible sense about the book that things have to end in crucifixion—for everybody.

In *Murder of Christ* there is much scorn towards the average man (whoever he is) and disgust, pitiless disgust. There is, as almost always, the reckless insistence on the possession of the inmost thoughts of everyone—which is the stuff, joy and torment of adolescence, the time before a person knows where to begin to respect the limits of another. There is outrage also, especially in the assertion that when you come down to it, all men think they are shit. But Reich does not convince me he means it.

There is also overpowering loneliness, even desolation. But that too is not really the tone I have been trying to recast. Something else was bothering Reich. I think it was disappointment in Creation, almost God's disappointment in Creation.

In part I think it was the dread which overcomes many creators after creation which took hold of Reich.

A waste, an emptiness—that waste and emptiness that haunted Tolstoy. There was also a sense that knowledge and words were not enough, even did not matter, that life went on without them in a thick, glowing silence, like the thick glowing silence of the bright sky. It was as if Reich doubted for the first time. As if he asked for the first time if what you learned and said made a difference, was in an important sense part of life, asked whether it was not more appropriate to keep silence. But how would he keep silence? It was as if he faltered in his boldness and asked himself if he could distinguish it from outrage.

There is none of the enthusiasm, with its readiness to minimize difficulties, of his preceding work. It was as if he now dreaded his earlier expectations and readiness to hope, as if it struck him now in the blows of memory as a waste of spirit in an expense of shame. He almost regretted. He allowed himself petty outcries about the time of his life he had sacrificed to his work and to the troubles of others. There was little of the hot indignation which had come with his hope, but much scorn of individuals, as if they had betrayed him. They could not create, they could not bring anything out of themselves but fed avidly on what the Prometheans (he did not use the word or image) brought them, what they did came to nothing and would come to nothing. They would learn, after many murderous wars laid their world to waste. The tone is savage, snarling, shocking. It amounts almost to cursing. But it also feels hurt and disappointed. There was something Reich saw clearly but could not acknowledge.

Who was he, after all, to say men disappointed him? Maybe he was on the edge of asking himself that.

I think what he saw but would not acknowledge was the integrity of the smallness of men. He began, I think, then, to sense that smallness did not of itself imply pettiness, that other men were not Titans like himself did not indicate they wanted, but feared to be, like himself, that some men chose to be small because they were actually small and that this did not necessarily imply they were little.

I mean Reich feared individuals. He feared the unique, feared what made one man in some sense entirely different from another. He was so ready to take responsibility for others, because in an important way he did not know how to take responsibility for himself, to live his own life instead of the life of everybody. This is usually the suffering of an artist. Again, I find myself reminding myself he was not an artist.

In fact Reich feared the unique in himself—as well as in others. As a result Reich tried to cope with his genius by sharing it with others, by teaching them how they could be like himself, if they dared. It was in part a way of coping with what was special about himself, that is with himself. His self embarrassed him: he wished to be without it and to live.

His presence could not bear an inadvertent awkwardness. He sensed the embarrassment of others with themselves and took it for an embarrassment with life itself. His loving touching of heaven and earth was a way of entering all nature, but his urgency in that entrance sprang from fear of himself and his own mortality.

Socrates, Christ coped with their genius by trying to let others be themselves. There is nothing more terrifying. In contrast, most men of genius know that the decision (probably necessarily conscious) to be true to their gifts requires the realization that they cannot be imparted to others who are without the same courage. Somehow Reich wanted it both ways: he wanted to be both like most men of genius and like Socrates and Christ. As a result in his freedom there is always some ambiguity about the distinction between himself and somebody else. Reich tried to obliterate this distinction by invoking the truth's preeminence, almost as if he was the only one who could speak for it. In face of the truth, what did the distinction between one individual and another matter? But the point about the truth is that it speaks for itself or not at all. It has no representatives.

Reich found it hard to see that many people did not dare, and more importantly, did not want to be like him. Maybe that was hardest of all to take, that many could do without his work, which for him meant always do without him.

FOOTNOTES

Footnotes

1. A. S. Neill, "Autobiography," *Journal of Orgonomy,* 2,2 (1968) 145-149, 147. See footnote 24.

2. David Blasband, "United States of America versus Wilhelm Reich," *JO* 1, 1-2, (1967) 56-130; for the United States Attorney, Peter Mills, who had previously represented Reich, 67. Cf. also D. Blasband, "United States of America Versus Wilhelm Reich (Part II)," *JO* 2,1, (1968) 24-67; R. Blasband, C. F. Rosenblum (pseudonym), D. Blasband, "An Analysis of the United States Food and Drug Administration's Scientific Evidence Against Wilhelm Reich," *JO* 6,2 (1972) 207-231; 7,2 (1973) 234-245; Jerome Greenfield, *Wilhelm Reich versus the U.S.A.,* New York: Norton, 1974.

3. Howard Fisher, "The Great Electrical Philosopher," published lecture, St. John's College, Annapolis, Md., 1976.

4. A.S. Neill, "The Man Reich," in David Boadella, *Wilhelm Reich: the Evolution of his Work,* New York: Dell, 1975, 389-397: "The presumptuous person made him wild, and any sign of insincerity or phoneyness made him see red."

5. "Der Orgasmus als electrophysiologische Entladung." *Zeitschrift fuer Politische Psychologie Sexualoekonomie* 1, 1934, 29-34. A translation of this article appears in *JO* 2,2 (1968), 117-131.Cf. also, *Experimentelle Ergebnisse ueber die Elektrische Funktion von Sexualitaet und Angst,* Copenhagen: Sexpolverlag, 1937; a translation of this study appears in *JO* 3, 1 (1969) 4-29 and in 3,2 (1969) 132-154. Work on the orgasm appears in *Character Analysis* (third English language edition, 1945; the first German language version, 1927), both of which are at present in print in two translations, of which the one by Theodore P. Wolfe, M.D. was done in cooperation with Reich. There is a bibliography complete until about 1953, including references to reviews of Reich's books, published by the Orgone Institute Press, Rangeley, Maine, in 1953 *(Wilhelm Reich: Biographical Material),* which is hard to obtain.

6. Myron Sharaf, "Some Remarks of Reich: Summer 1948," *JO* 3,1 (1969) 116-119, especially 119.

7. For Reich's account of his struggle with Freud, *Reich Speaks of Freud,* New York: Farrar, Straus and Giroux, 1967.

8. For the work on energy, *Die Bione, Klinische und experimentelle Berichte,* Oslo, Sexpolverlag, 1938; English translation, Derek Eastmond, Nottingham, Ritter Press, 1948, 1970; another translation of *Die Bione* was scheduled to begin appearing in *JO* 10, 1, 1976. Also, *The Discovery of the Orgone,* I. *Function of the Orgasm,* 2 New York, 1948; *The Discovery of the Orgone,* II. *The Cancer Biopathy,* New York, 1948; *Cosmic Superimposition, Man's Orgonotic Roots in Nature,* Rangeley, Maine, 1951. All the English language editions of these works are in print.

9. Sheila Ostrander and Lynn T. Schroeder, *Psychic Dis-*

coveries Behind the Iron Curtain, New York, Prentice-Hall, 1970; for a consideration of the relations of the Soviet work to Reich's, Trevor James Constable, JO 5,2, 1971, 221-225.

10. The Oranur Experiment—First Report (1947-1951), Rangeley, Maine: Orgone Institute Press, 1951.

11. For Reich's membership in the Communist party, Arthur Koestler, The God That Failed, New York; Harper, 1949, 43; Reich, People in Trouble, Rangeley, Maine: Orgone Institute Press, 1953, 21, 131, and elsewhere.

12. Elsworth F. Baker, Man in the Trap, New York: Macmillan, 1967, 68.

13. Elsworth F. Baker, Man in the Trap, New York, 1967, 223 and elsewhere.

14. See footnote 2 for writings on Reich's prosecution.

15. Orson Bean, Me and the Orgone, New York: St. Martin's, 1971; Alexander Lowen, Bioenergetics, New York: Coward McCann, 1975.

16. Myron Sharaf, "Further Remarks of Reich: 1949," JO 7,1 (1973) 116.

17. For this work on vision, Elsworth F. Baker, Man in the Trap, New York, 1967, 16-20.

18. For the antithesis between mystical and mechanistic thinking, Reich, Ether, God and Devil, Rangeley, Maine: Orgone Institute Press, 1951.

19. For some more discussion of the expurgations in regard to The Invasion of Compulsory Sex-Morality (first German language edition, 1932; first English language

publication, 1971), Leo Raditsa, "Reich's Search for Freedom,' *The New Leader* 54 (1971) 24ff.

20. I have lost the reference to the remark of Reich's about his mother. For Reich's relation to his mother, Ilse Ollendorff Reich, *Wilhelm Reich: A Personal Biography,* New York: St. Martin's 3; Lois Wyvell, "An Appreciation of Reich," *JO* 7,2 (1973) 177-186, especially 173-74.

21. For one, of many, descriptions of attitudes in totalitarian societies, Mikhail Agursky, "Contemporary Socioeconomic Systems and their Future Prospects," in *From Under the Rubble* (ed. Alexander Solzhenitsyn), Boston: Little, Brown, 1975.

22. *Hope Against Hope,* New York: Atheneum, 1970, 289.

23. For Reich on consciousness, *Cosmic Superimposition,* Rangeley, Maine, 1951, 101-121, especially 114-121.

24. In 1948 Reich remarked to A.S. Neill, "I wish to God you lived in America; I have no one to talk to; the men around me are my patients." A.S. Neill, "Autobiography," *JO* 2,2 (1968), 147.

25. See footnote 17.

26. A.S. Neill's comment:

> Reich always put up a barrier. He addressed his fellow workers as Dr. X or Dr. Y and they addressed him as Dr. Reich. I think that Ola Raknes, of Oslo, and I were the only friends and co-workers who addressed him simply as Reich. He never called me, "Mister." I challenged him about his attitude of standoffishness. His defence was: *"In this work familiarity with me could destroy it. They would encroach on me emotionally."* "But, Reich," I

said, "I've been plain Neill to adults and pupils for thirty-five years and no one has abused the privilege of dropping my title." "You are different," he replied. "You aren't handling dynamite as I am doing. I am attacking the whole anti-life armouring of modern man and man will kill me if he can." Man did in the end. (Underlining mine.)

A.S. Neill, "The Man Reich" in David Boadella, *Wilhelm Reich,* New York, 1975, 53.

27. Ilse Ollendorff Reich, *Wilhelm Reich: A Personal Biography,* New York: St. Martin's, 1969, 53.

28. Ilse Ollendorff Reich, *Wilhelm Reich,* New York, 1969, 5, 28.

29. The only published account of this tragedy is in Ilse Ollendorff Reich, *Wilhelm Reich,* New York, 1969, 3-5. For comments on this account, Myron Sharaf, *JO* 3,2 (1969), 254-266.

30. Ilse Ollendorff Reich (*Wilhelm Reich*, New York, 1969,3) writes:

Reich talked very little about his relationship with his father. I have the feeling that it was a very ambivalent relationship, because on more than one occasion Reich tried to imply that he was not really his father's son, that maybe his mother had a relationship with one of the Ukranian peasants—a rather unlikely story for that time and place—and in the end, went so far as to offer the even more unlikely proposition that he was the offspring of his mother and a man from outer space.

The detail about coming from outer space also appears in Reich's last published work, *Contact with Space: the second Oranur Report,* New York: Core Pilot Press, 1957 (not easily available).

31. *The Murder of Christ,* Rangeley, Maine: Orgone Institute Press, 1953 (written in 1951), in print at present.

32. *Listen, Little Man!* Rangeley, Maine: Orgone Institute Press, 1948, in print at present.